# The Vision
# and
# God's Providence

Distributed by
Hartland Publications
Box 1
Rapidan, VA 22733

ISBN   0-923309-91-8

# The Vision
# and
# God's Providence

by Colin Standish
President, Hartland Institute

Hartland Publications
Rapidan, VA 22733

# The Vision and God's Providence

# Foreword

by Russell Standish

Dawn had broken on a magnificent October morning. Long shadows of the forest trees formed across the large, verdant, well-manicured lawn fronting the magnificent Southern mansion gracing the property. The rays of the sun struck the eight sandstone pillars which signify the entrance to the gracious building, displaying them after the disguise of night darkness dispersed. What a sight!

The seven hundred sixty acre property upon which this mansion rests at the apex of a gentle incline was surely a precinct in which the Holy Spirit walked and rested in the hearts of the staff, students and the potential Wellness Center guests. It was surrounded upon two sides by the Robinson River, crafted out of the picturesque Piedmont Valley of Virginia, eighty miles southwest of Washington D.C.

As I viewed this scene for the first time in October, 1983, only three months after Hartland Institute had been established, I marvelled at God's goodness, His love for the small band of humble, yet highly qualified workers who had covenanted to establish an institution to the glory of God, to promote the completion of the work of God on this sin-cursed earth.

Here was a faint but beautiful and tranquil reflection of Eden. Shortly, as the sun rose higher in the clear blue sky, I observed a panorama which could not be a replica of Eden, yet was a scene of marked beauty. The forest, with leaves painted in Autumn tones, the ambers, the rich reds, vivid yellows and many other subtle hues and tints, presented a breathtaking vista.

Shortly, the squirrels and chipmunks were scampering to forage for food. The occasional deer leapt deftly through the forest. I was to discover that Hartland was a zoo without any restrictive fences whatsoever, an aviary without a cage: it was an arboretum crafted by nature and created by God.

The migrating Canada geese choosing to hatch their young at the five lakes on the property have proven to be a sight of much interest. The cardinal birds, the robins and blue jays producing flashes of color in the woods, enlivening the scene, never lose their interest. Nor do the skunks who considerately seldom perfume the air, the raccoons, and the occasional black bear ambling harmlessly across the property, lose their fascination.

Only God could have found such a haven for His people. The faith of those sacrificing pioneers has been amply rewarded. As I have met consecrated young men and women from every continent and many nations returning to their homelands fired with the zeal of the Lord, their talents greatly advanced by a training designed in spiritual and intellectual excellence, I praised God that He has poured His blessing upon that which He designed.

Hartland has stood, and continues to stand, as a bastion for the teaching of Bible truths and principles. It is now fifty-one years since I first entered upon my own work for God. I have never in that period visited one training school to equal Hartland College upon any of the world's continents. It is balanced; it is true to inspired counsels; it produces graduates whose minds have been expanded by the study of the Word. I have seen young men and women of apparently limited potential come forth from Hartland as giants in the cause of God. On the other hand, I have seen promising young people enter other colleges, only to graduate as spiritual and intellectual pygmies.

The reason for Hartland's ascendancy is not difficult to discern.

Used as a textbook in our schools, the Bible will do for the mind and morals what cannot be done by books of science and philosophy.
—*CT* 422

The study of the Bible is superior to all other study in strengthening the intellect. —*MYP* 253

Hartland College bears full testimony to the accuracy of these statements. The evidence is clear for all to see. Two decades of the implementation of these principles in Hartland College proved a longitudinal study which provides evidence beyond dispute of the excellence of its training.

I have seen over this period the expanding of Hartland's work. The well-equipped and well-staffed Wellness Center provides a first-class means of gaining and maintaining physical, mental and emotional strength. Its program is based upon sound biblical and physiological principles. I personally have benefited greatly from attending this program on two occasions a decade apart. As a physician I carefully evaluated the principles used. They were sound and free from faulted "natural" health cures and practices so frequently found in health institutions. Numerous health guests have experiences which provide testimony confirming my own.

The development of Hartland World Mission has directed staff and students to many corners of the earth, proclaiming the gospel of salvation.

Numerous souls have been won to Christ from these outreaches.

Hartland Publications has reached maturity as a publishing house which can be trusted to provide books, audio tapes, CDs and video tapes of the highest quality. It is superior to any other book center I have visited in its careful selection of materials for sale.

And then there are the Hartland Camp Meetings and Convocations, the largest such self-supporting meetings in the western world. It has been my privilege to present God's truths in many of these meetings. The believers who attend are not only numerous, but among the most committed Seventh-day Adventists I have ever met. Despite Hartland's distance from major cities, God's people come from the far reaches of the United States and Canada to be filled with the Spirit of truth and to savor holy fellowship with God's people.

I have seen God's blessing in other ways. The building of the Wellness Center, the Hartland Publications headquarters, the male students' dormitories, many staff residences, the large meeting pavilion, the toilet-and-shower block, and the paving of about three miles of roads within the property all testify to God's care and the love and generous support of God's people.

Important as these improvements are, they pale in comparison to the mighty witness of Hartland in the cause of truth. The value of the souls won to the truth is beyond estimation. The steady stand for God's Word and the principles of His faith in an age of gross apostasy; the continuing graduation of an army of youth rightly trained to complete the greatest task to which man has been called; those who have followed the inspired principles enunciated by the institution; the books and magazines distributed proclaiming truth; the pastoral care of God's flock in the dedication of children; the conducting of funerals; the anointing of the sick; baptisms performed; marriages consecrated; presentation of revival meetings; solemn counsels provided; communion services conducted; these and many other acts of care will not be fully measured until heaven provides a complete reckoning.

One day—a day nigh at hand—Hartland's work will be completed. The dawn will be broken by rays of sunshine for the final time. For the last time western skies across the valley will be painted in sunset hues. Hartland will be a pile of rubble, its outreach no longer required, its staff and students scattered. In Earth's darkest hour, at His glorious appearing, our Lord will take His faithful servants home.

This transcendent event will not write the final chapter in the history of Hartland. In the Book of Remembrance, which God has immortalized, will be the record of sacrificial service, fidelity to God of a quality unusual in an age of unprecedented faithlessness and wickedness. Souls rescued from the pit of sin, believers encouraged and strengthened, a worldwide witness to Christ, His incomparable salvation and the treasures, joy and privileges of eternity, these and much more will constitute a large entry in that Book.

For now we look with longing desire for that day, and praise our Redeemer that in the few moments of probationary time remaining, He has called faithful, humble believers to be His servants in Hartland's mission which circles the planet.

# ACKNOWLEDGEMENTS

It is with deep gratitude that I acknowledge the special help and contributions to the preparation of this book. Brother Hal Mayer has been of great assistance helping me to detail events either forgotten or of which I had only partial recollection. He also offered editorial suggestions.

Also of great help has been my brother, Russell, who has reviewed the manuscript and offered not only editorial changes, but has suggested several areas to be included in the body of the text of this book. He also kindly wrote the beautifully crafted Foreword to this book.

Sister Daphne Corey has toiled patiently in preparing the manuscript for publication. She has worked through many revisions, additions and alterations while offering suggestions of suitable changes of expression from time to time. She also has done much research to fill in details of this manuscript.

For the help of many others I am also very appreciative.

C.S.

# DEDICATION

This book is dedicated to the pioneers of Hartland Instutitute: the Board of Trustees, staff, students, guests, and the contributors who have prayed, donated finances and equipment, and volunteered time to provide practical help for all the needs of the Institute and inspired the development and expansion of its ministry.

Above all, this book is dedicated to the One who alone has inspired and provided for Hartland's every need.

# 1     The Vision

*Where there is no vision, the people perish: but he that keepeth the law, happy is he.*            —Proverbs 29:18

THE story of Hartland Institute is the story of the struggles and triumphs, the fear and faith, the failures and successes, the timidity and courage, and the hesitations and visions of fallible men and women. In spite of human limitations, the glorious power of the Almighty God has been revealed.

Not simply the achievements or accomplishments of men or women can tell the story of the initial or subsequent development of Hartland Institute, for its foundation must be attributed to God alone. Yet many men and women have had the privilege of being His humble instruments to contribute to Hartland's establishment. Some worked as the pioneer Hartland team. Others have come to continue the Institute's development, while yet others have supported Hartland's vision with prayers, encouraging words, or have given direction as constituents and Board members and by serving on Advisory Committees. Still others have contributed funds, equipment and labor. All who have assisted over the years have been crucial for the construction of a mosaic which represents an example of God's artwork. Some have passed to their rest. We honor their memory.

As this book recalls divine leadings, it may at times appear as if the development had been largely free from struggle, human weakness, misunderstandings, and strong differences of opinion. All these human frailties occurred, and we cannot but wonder what God might have accomplished, had we listened perfectly to His voice. Yet despite human weakness, there has been much faith, prayer and soul searching which God has honored.

We are told that "we have nothing to fear for the future, except as we shall forget the way the Lord has led us, and His teaching in our past history" (*Selected Messages*, Bk. 3, p. 162). With this thought, I pray that Hartland's upward development, following the plan of God, will be interrupted only by the close of human probation. My vision is that the members of the Hartland family—staff, students, and guests—will contribute mightily to the hastening of that day.

"What are your plans for the future?" Little did I realize the far-reaching implications of this casual question. I had flown to Philadelphia from Sacramento in February, 1982. At the time, I was Dean of Weimar College, which I had helped establish in 1978. Two of the first students, Hal Mayer and Greg Harper, comprised the first graduating class in the summer of 1981. Greg accepted a call to pastor in the Nevada-Utah Conference.

The Seventh-day Adventist church was founded partially by youths with vision. Hal Mayer, nearing his mid-twenties by the time he graduated from Weimar College, also possessed a vision. He set the wheels in motion with a plan to begin a health-conditioning center near Hamburg, Pennsylvania, where his parents owned a large nursing home. Energized by his experience at Weimar, he dreamed of a similar institution on the East Coast.

Hal organized weekend seminars at Blue Mountain Academy, where health, educational, and spiritual themes were presented. In the first three seminars, men associated with Weimar Institute were the main speakers: Elder Dick Winn, Dr. George Chen and me. Obviously, Hal's enthusiasm had spread and many asked, "Why is there not a Weimar in the East?"

*Health Ministries East* was established as a base. This new organization immediately began publishing a bimonthly paper, *Breakthrough*. With the generous assistance of *American Cassette Ministries'* mailing list, *Breakthrough* was sent to over 10,000 homes.

Early in 1982 Brother Mayer contacted me asking if I would be willing to conduct an education seminar at Blue Mountain Academy. It was arranged for February of that year. A group of more than sixty people attended the seminar. It was on the journey from Philadelphia airport to Hamburg, Pennsylvania, that I asked the question, "What are your plans for the future?" Hal responded that he was interested in establishing a health center, possibly in Pennsylvania, after the lines of the Newstart Center at Weimar. This led to my follow-up question, "Have you ever thought of combining an educational facility with the health center?" Hal responded enthusiastically to this expansion of his original vision. In between the education seminars, which were well received, Hal and I dialogued upon the great need of such a center on the East Coast of the United States.

By this time I knew Hal well. While I was president of Columbia Union College he studied respiratory therapy there, graduating in 1978. When I accepted the call to Weimar he was one of a number of students who showed a significant interest in training there. However, of those interested, Hal was the only one who actually came to Weimar, where he took a composite degree in health ministry—a combination of training for the ministry and health education. It was from this composite major that he graduated in 1981. He had shown himself to be very active in outreach ministry and, with Greg Harper, he had become an elder at a young age in the Truckee Church in eastern California, a constituent church of the Nevada-Utah conference. These two young men had needed to shoulder heavy responsibilities when the head elder was unable to continue his leadership role.

The concept of an education and health ministry on the East Coast began to gather interest and support. It was then decided that on July 25, 1982, a Sunday afternoon meeting would be held at Blue Mountain Academy to explore the extent of interest in such an institution.

Immediately prior to this meeting my wife and I had traveled to Crieff in Scotland where a combined health and retirement facility was operated by Seventh-day Adventists. At that time there was a suggestion that Weimar might administer that institution. However, this possibility ultimately did not eventuate. It was from Britain that we returned to the United States East Coast in late July. I proceeded to Hamburg for an exploratory meeting.

Dr. Dennis Blum, Dr. Raymond Moore and I traveled to Blue Mountain Academy, purposing to test the interest of eastern Seventh-day Adventists in developing a significant self-supporting health and education center for the Eastern United States.

We were well pleased at the inaugural meeting to find that the gathered people represented states from Maine to Florida. I had been asked to chair the meeting. The agenda was fluid. The central question of course was, "Would there be a strong enough interest on the East Coast for the establishment of a educational-health center?" After considerable time in dialogue, we took a secret ballot of all who were present, asking if they believed that God would support such an institution.

It was proposed that this institution would be established upon the God-given principles of the Bible and the writings of Sister Ellen White. The new institution would be designed to help fulfill two prophecies of Sister White: 1) That before the close of probation educational institutions of a "different order" (*Counsels to Parents, Teachers, and Students*, p. 532) would be established, and 2) it was also agreed to follow the divine pattern by opening a health-conditioning center in combination with the college program. The organizers understood that the final work for mankind would center around medical missionary service, thus linking together two great arms of the Church. Of the one hundred and twenty-two people present at the meeting, one hundred and twenty-one said, "Yes," and one indicated he or she was uncertain. No one voted, "No."

With that confirmation, we then asked what those present could contribute to the resources of such an institution. When the papers were gathered up over $30,000 had been pledged, plus a variety of pieces of equipment helpful to such an institution. One does not have to be an educator or a health professional to see the limitations of this financial basis for establishing an institution, but there was a very strong enthusiasm for the project and we were impressed that God was moving us forward in faith.

During this meeting an interim Board of Directors was chosen to guide the task force in developing the new institution. The members chosen were: Glenn Hoffman (New Jersey), Chairman; Colin Standish (California), Vice Chairman; Hal Mayer (Pennsylvania); Lester Ortiz (Pennsylvania); Darwin Heisey (Pennsylvania); Josephine Cunnington Edwards (Pennsylvania), James Drexler (Maine), and Raymond Moore (Michigan).

At this time there was no money in hand, no chosen location, no facilities, no equipment and no staff. Yet in faith those gathered urged that this institution be commenced on July 1, 1983, giving little more than eleven months for an immense amount of work to be accomplished. It was argued that it was necessary to commence quickly so that potential supporters would gain confidence in the likely success of the project. Rightly it was concluded that long delays would lead to a diminution of interest and support for the proposed institution.

That same afternoon the interim board of directors met under the chairmanship of Glenn Hoffman, of New Jersey. I was amazed at the determination with which this board addressed its responsibilities. It was unanimously decided that we should look for a rural property within range of a major East Coast city. The target city initially chosen was New York City, with a proposed location in northern New Jersey.

The interim board then moved quickly to discuss leadership. The members expressed a belief that without a chosen leader the project was not likely to proceed with due haste. The focus was directed to me and the question was asked, "Would you be willing to come back to the East Coast and lead this new institution?" I was given little time to ponder this question, but I believe the Lord guided me in my response.

I had, during my ministry, always taken the position that if an invitation or call reached me, I would accept it. This had led me to Burringbar and Mullumbimby, both primary (elementary) schools in Australia, Avondale College, West Indies College, Columbia Union College and Weimar Institute. However, I knew the responsibilities of leading in the commencement of yet another institution would be weighty. I desired to be sure that the Lord was in this call. When I accepted the call to Weimar I had the knowledge that at least that institution had begun to operate a health center. Here, however, we were without any tangible evidence that such a project would be commenced, much less survive.

I was familiar with the forecast that the 1980s would be a very difficult period in which to start a post-secondary institution because available students were predicted to be considerably fewer than during the 1970s.

After a brief pause I informed the board I could not respond to that invitation until I was satisfied by the board's answer to two questions: (1) "Will truth be the *summum bonum* (the highest good) in any such institution?" I explained that I had served in too many institutions where truth was not held supreme. I pressed my conviction that if truth were not the highest order, then we would fail both in our educational and health ministry goals. I had no interest in serving in an institution unless the preservation of the truth of the three angels' messages and the everlasting gospel would pervade everything undertaken in the institution.

The resounding unanimous support for this principle led me to my second question: (2) "Will this new institution and its board stand resolutely against any form of human accreditation?" I explained that if I were to take this heavy responsibility in the uncharted waters ahead, I was determined that the only voice to which I desired to listen was the voice of God. Once again, with resolute unanimity the board accepted this condition. Of course this goal in no wise excluded wide counseling with godly men and women. I believed the Lord was calling and I accepted the invitation. In the more than twenty years which have followed I have never once doubted that this call was of God.

At the same meeting the interim Board accepted the gracious offer tendered by Dr. Raymond Moore to use Hewitt Research Foundation, of which he was president, to be a conduit for donations to the new institution, until we were able to secure our own nonprofit organizational tax status—the 501-c-3 Federal Tax classification.

# 2 The Search

*And I say unto you, Ask, and it shall be given you; seek, and
ye shall find; knock, and it shall be opened unto you.*
—Luke 11:9

HE morning following the meeting at Blue Mountain Academy
was a vigorous planning session for Dennis Blum, Hal Mayer and
myself. The east coast is a huge stretch of territory, almost two
thousand miles from the northern tip of Maine to the Florida Keys. The
first target state was New Jersey. Already a beautiful property had been
identified in the New Jersey woodlands within thirty miles of downtown
Manhattan, yet so rural was the environment that it could have been a
thousand miles away. The property had been the leadership training headquarters of the Boy Scouts of America. However, when we expressed
an interest in it, we discovered that it was owned by the big telecommuni-
cation corporation, AT&T, which had decided to sell it because of strong
community opposition to its plan to develop the property into a corporate
training center.

The afternoon after the inaugural meeting, a group traveled to northern New Jersey to meet with representatives of AT&T. We had hoped
that they would show an interest in donating the property to our project
for a tax write-off. The property had been listed at 5.8 million dollars. It
seemed almost perfect for what we desired, with many buildings and
facilities which would be suitable for dormitories, cafeteria and housing.
However, the AT&T representative showed no interest whatsoever in
such a proposal.

We had prayed most earnestly before taking part in the meeting, and
we were somewhat uncertain as to the next move we should take. We
made the decision to visit with the Director of Higher Education for the
State of New Jersey the following morning. It took little time for us to
understand that New Jersey was not the state the Lord had chosen for
this new institution. This understanding helped us to realize why there
was no opening to acquire the beautiful New Jersey property. After the
first response of the Director to my opening question, I knew that New
Jersey was not our target state.

My first question was, "How many categories do you have for operating a college in the State of New Jersey?" Her answer was, "Only

one." We could have left at that point, because we knew that limitation would involve either state approval or regional accreditation, and we were seeking a state which would permit us the freedom to be exempted from accreditation and state certification. But the only status offered in New Jersey was, "state approval."

The Interim Board had already determined that the new institute would not be subservient to the state or to any accrediting body. This board desired the very highest standard of Christian education, not the faulted standards of those who knew not God's paradigm. Under its rules, the State of New Jersey possessed the legal right to determine curriculum and to monitor the program closely during its development and continuing operation, conditions unacceptable to the planners of the new institution.

The Board of Directors had agreed to listen to but one voice—the voice of God—in directing the entire program of the new institute. There was a conscious covenant to follow God's education and health plans without interference from a state or other human organization. The die was cast: New Jersey would not be the location for the new institute.

I was taken by surprise by the New Jersey restriction to a single category because, being situated at Weimar at the time, I was aware that in California there were four categories for operating a college: (1) state approval, (2) regional accreditation, (3) state authorization, or (4) Bible college. Before I arrived at Weimar the leaders had chosen the state authorization category. I was disappointed that they had not chosen the Bible college option, because that would have provided complete freedom from any outside control. At first the authorization category involved no state interference, but later, as I predicted could happen, increasing criteria were added by the State, causing Weimar many difficulties in subsequent years.

Realizing that the East Coast was strikingly different from the West Coast, or at least from California, we decided to telephone many of the Higher Education Departments of the states on the United States East Coast. I telephoned New Hampshire, Vermont, Massachusetts, Rhode Island, Connecticut, New York, Pennsylvania, Delaware, Maryland, District of Columbia, West Virginia and Virginia. I was shocked to discover that almost all had no religious exemption category of any kind. Pennsylvania and Maryland required that half-million dollars be placed in an escrow account with the Department of Higher Education before any consideration would be given to an application to establish a new college. We had virtually no financial resources, so immediately those states were placed outside our focus. All other states, too, were unacceptable, with the exception of Virginia. In West Virginia the director explained that they were considering some category for religious exemption, but we could not wait to see whether or not West Virginia would pass such laws. To the best of my knowledge they have not yet done so.

How we thank the Lord for Thomas Jefferson, whose extensive influence in the Commonwealth of Virginia Statehouse had been successful in the passage of a bill which provided for the religious exemption category in order that religious education institutions might be established. We later discovered that this category has been rarely sought in the history of the Commonwealth, but was still available. We had now found a home for God's new institution. Brother Mayer and I hastened to Richmond, the state capital in order to dialogue with the officials in the Departments of Higher Education and Health, for our desire was to operate both a college and a health center.

We were amazed with his response when we spoke to the Higher Education Director, John Molnar. We asked him for the details required to apply for the religious exemption category. He simply said, "Here are the forms, fill them out." I then pressed him, expecting that there would be certain criteria which would have to be met to guarantee that we would operate a religious college. He again reiterated, "All you are required to do is to fill out the forms and file them, stating that you will take the religious exemption status." Persisting a little further I asked, "What happens if we prove not to be religious?" He responded, "We are too busy caring for the state colleges and universities in Virginia to be concerned about how religious your college will be." And then as if in a postscript, he said, "I guess if we had a real objection from someone we might have to investigate."

Later, however, he added two criteria wholly consistent with our goals: (1) that all majors we would offer contain wording to show that they had a religious foundation. He agreed that if they contained words such as "evangelism," "Christian," "ministry," "theology" and other obviously religious words, the requirement would be satisfied. (2) That the diplomas we would issue to our graduates have a clear statement that the college was not state-approved. I asked if we might simply state, "Hartland College has chosen not to accept state approval." He informed us that would be fine. God truly was leading.

God had directed us to the State where the new institution would be located, and when we contemplated upon this fact we perceived many advantages. Virginia is almost halfway between Maine and Florida. Virginia is in the South and therefore we were in a "right-to-work" state (meaning that citizens have the right to work without joining a labor union). As a southern state Virginia, generally speaking, has lower costs than the northern states, especially in respect of property and building costs.

We now focused upon an intensive search for a suitable property. Because I was still busily engaged as dean of the college at Weimar, I could not participate personally in this search, which became the responsibility of the relatively newly married couple, Hal and Betsy Mayer. We discussed the criteria in the Spirit of Prophecy for the location of a college—first, it must be located in a rural area, close enough to population centers that we could carry on a vigorous outreach ministry. Second, the desired location was to be within reasonable range of an airport and public forms of transportation. Third, the property should have many buildings already erected on it so that we could commence quickly. Fourth, there would need to be a good supply of water; and finally, that there be land suitable for agriculture.

Through the generosity of Hal's parents, Laurena and Richard Mayer, Hal and Betsy were provided the use of their recreational vehicle to travel south of Washington to the northern and central regions of Virginia, which we now targeted for the location of the new institution. Washington, D.C. was the major metropolitan area upon which we now focused for city missionary work. The Mayers were shown many beautiful plantations which lacked but one quality; significant numbers of buildings.

One day Brother Hal Mayer was waiting in the office of Art Palmer, a realtor in the town of Warrenton. As Brother Mayer was browsing through the brochures of various available properties, he noticed a large brochure detailing the features of Hartland Hall Plantation. He observed that it had eleven hundred and ninety-two acres, on which was a large mansion, a manor house, and fourteen other homes. His excitement was difficult to contain, and when the realtor appeared Hal inquired about the property. The realtor said, "I don't think you would be interested in that property. The buildings are dilapidated and falling down. It hasn't been lived in for a long time. Besides, its down there in Madison County where there are only ten thousand people. It is not in a sophisticated county like we have here in Fauquier County." The more he said, the more interested Brother Mayer became. He responded, "Let us see this property." So with a level of reluctance the realtor took Brother Mayer to Hartland Hall Plantation.

Later in the day I received a telephone call from an excited Brother Mayer telling me about this property and asking if I could fly out in the foreseeable future to inspect it. Making speedy plans, I was able to visit the property before the end of October, 1982. The Lord had promised in the Spirit of Prophecy that properties already considerably developed would be available for purchase at well below their real value, as was this site. Yet not until some time later was the Board convinced that this property was the one the Lord had chosen.

> The opportunity to purchase this church property is one fulfillment of the light given me by the Lord that to our people would be offered at a price far below the original cost, properties that could be used in our work.                    —*Review and Herald*, September 7, 1905

God had directed us not only to Virginia, but also to the property. It was now nearing the end of 1982. Would Hartland reach the expectation of the members of the initial meeting and be ready to commence July 1, 1983, a little more than six months away? More importantly, the questions in our minds were, how would we accumulate the funds necessary to purchase such a property? And where would we find suitable staff?

# 3     The Decision

*It is even more excusable to make a wrong decision sometimes than to be continually in a wavering position, to be hesitating, sometimes inclined in one direction, then in another. More perplexity and wretchedness result from thus hesitating and doubting than from sometimes moving too hastily.*
*—Testimonies for the Church*, Vol. 3, p. 497

ALTHOUGH Hartland Hall Plantation seemed a promising property, it was not yet actually decided that this would be the property upon which the health and educational institution would be established. The academic break toward the end of December provided opportunity for a serious decision to be contemplated. It was decided to put aside about ten days to help make this decision. Ken Glantz, (a former county building inspector in Oregon, then Director of Plant Services at Weimar Institute), Dennis Blum (designated to be Dean of the college when established), and I traveled from Sacramento to Washington to help make a settled decision concerning the Hartland property or any others which might yet be worthy of our consideration.

On the first Sabbath, I preached at the Orange Church, eight miles south of Hartland Hall Plantation, and there for the first time shared the possibilities which we were contemplating. As Orange Church held its church service at nine-thirty in the morning, it was possible for me also to travel to the Culpeper Church, twelve miles north of Hartland Hall Plantation, to share with that congregation the possibilities concerning the establishment of an institution nearby. The members of both churches warmly responded to the thought that possibly such an institution would be established in that region of Virginia. At that time Pastor Willis Hackett, a retired vice-president of the General Conference, whom I knew reasonably well, was pastoring the Orange church, and he expressed very strong support for such a project.

We had invited about thirty brethren and sisters to meet with us the second weekend (New Year's weekend) for counsel and guidance focusing upon the direction in which we should move. Generally speaking this group consisted of business men and women whom we felt could provide wise counsel. However, there was much to do before we would meet with them in De Vivies Motel in Orange. We had not settled upon the property of Hartland Hall Plantation, though it certainly was a major focus. Hal Mayer had arranged a number of other visitations to properties within the area which were also available for sale. All of them were lovely plantations and had, in many ways, more eye appeal than did Hartland Hall Plantation. Those who have visited Hartland Institute will not comprehend why, in many ways, it looked so unattractive when we visited it. What a mess it was! There had been seven years of almost total neglect resulting in frozen and burst water pipes in the mansion. The ceilings and many of the walls were terribly dilapidated. The grass that had once been the lawns of the property was two feet or more high. The formal garden was almost indiscernible. A poor class of people lived in the various homes on a month-by-month rental basis. The beautiful grounds and property which visitors now witness bear little resemblance to what we viewed when we first visited the property. Only in our imagination could we conceive its beauty which became manifest after much effort to repair and to restore.

We were undecided what to do. "I think we should ask the Advisory Committee on Friday to decide between three properties here in North Central Virginia," I suggested on Wednesday of Christmas week, 1982. Dr. Dennis Blum, Hal and Betsy Mayer, Ken Glantz and I were still searching. All tended to agree, yet all of us were somehow troubled by the indecision. We had spent most of a week evaluating the options. How could we expect a committee to evaluate fully a number of properties in one short winter Friday?

Ken, whose vast construction knowledge was invaluable, took some of his vacation time to help in assessing the various properties. None others of the group had the necessary experience in this area. Ken confirmed the structural soundness of the Hartland mansion, yet the group still hesitated. Virginia seemed to be full of magnificent rural prop-erties, many of them much better manicured than Hartland Hall Planta-tion. The group realized that the suggestion, to ask the Committee to decide, was a way to avoid our responsibility. None relished making this tough decision. Yet, we finally understood that God had called us to narrow the choices. In a few short hours the Advisory Committee could not be expected to make the decision which this group had been unable to make in several months. Now was the hour of decision!

During the time of extensive reviewing and searching, Hal and Betsy Mayer stayed in motels while the three men stayed in the senior Mayer's recreational vehicle. One night after the Mayers had retired to their motel room and Dennis Blum, who was fighting influenza, had repaired to bed, Ken Glantz and I sat down to discuss options. Ken had carefully reviewed the Hartland Hall Plantation mansion and, in spite of all the cosmetic defects, he said it was magnificently built, almost like a fortress, and was a very valuable property. As we talked together I asked Ken if he would evaluate with me the cost for Hartland Hall Plantation to have the minimum buildings which we thought we would need in the future for such an institution as we planned. Then we compared those costs for the other two fine plantations which we were considering. We wished to compare the proverbial "apples with apples."

After a couple of hours of estimations, we came to the conclusion that Hartland Hall Plantation would cost about 1.2 million dollars less than either of the other properties to become a fully functioning institution. Our minds were settled. The following morning we met with the Mayers and Dennis Blum. We shared with them the data we had researched and our conclusions, and unanimity settled upon us. As we prayed together we were convicted that there was no purpose in looking at any other property, for we were convinced that God was leading us to Hartland Hall Plantation. Our decision was to recommend only one property—Hartland Hall Plantation—to the counselors and advisors.

Soon after we had made this decision, two other realtors arrived to take us to view other properties which they had searched out. However we told them that it would be a waste of their time and our time to visit these properties because we now had made our decision. We explained that unless these new properties could be established into a college less expensively than Hartland Hall Plantation, we would not be interested in visiting them. The realtors concurred that it would cost much more to establish all the additional buildings needed for the operation of the college, the wellness center and homes and other facilities at another location. God had used realtors to confirm our decision. Our recommendation was now set in concrete. However, it would not be finalized until after the meeting with the counselors.

The counselors gathered on Thursday evening at the motel. The plan was to have a meeting Friday morning, after which we planned a visit to Hartland Hall Plantation to seek the evaluation of these counselors upon the suitability of the property and its value. In a mighty way, God gave us on Thursday night a clear evidence of His blessing upon the project. We had invited Brother O. D. McKee, of McKee Bakery in Tennessee, to be present at this meeting. However, he called to say that his responsibilities would not allow him to be with us at the meeting. At first this appeared to be a very serious blow to our hopes. But in the course of our conversation Mr. McKee said, "Though I cannot be with you, we have decided to dedicate $150,000 to the project." Can you imagine our joy when we learned this? God was guiding and leading mightily, and this knowledge led to a season of prayer, thanking God for His blessings.

On Friday morning, we spent several hours discussing the vision, the goal, the objectives and the purposes of the proposed institution with the advisors. Questions were asked and uncertainties were clarified among the group present. We then traveled about nine miles to Hartland Hall Plantation, which was still in its unkempt condition. We wondered what impact this would have upon shrewd businessmen and other advisors. However, after we had surveyed the campus, toured through the mansion and explored the likely areas where future buildings would be established, we were pleasantly surprised to receive a general consensus of approval for this property. Like us, this ad hoc group of business people had seen the potential of the property. After this we repaired to our various places of abode and prepared for the Sabbath.

Early Sabbath morning I traveled with a number of our interested people to Richmond, where I had the opportunity to preach in the Patterson Avenue Church. Again there was great interest in the concept of a health-educational institute in Virginia.

Saturday night and Sunday morning we planned a business meeting with the counselors from Maine to Florida and from the West Coast. Also present were members of the Board of Directors and a number who were likely to serve at the Institute. This meeting was held in the fellowship hall at Burnt Mills Seventh-day Adventist Church in Maryland. Again the consensus was that Hartland Hall Plantation was the property we should vigorously pursue as the location for this new ministry.

We asked those present to pledge their financial support for this ministry. We were disappointed: the amount pledged was less than $37,000. We had hoped for much more. No doubt these business people were cautious of financial commitments until something substantial was underway. Yet we were not discouraged, because still fresh in our minds was the pledge made by Mr. O. D. McKee.

We sought counsel on how much to offer for the five hundred acres comprising the northeastern section of the property. Before making the decision we gathered in small groups for prayer. As we prayed a unifying spirit came upon us. One of the lady advisors suggested $750,000. Immediately others declared they had been thinking the same amount, although we knew it to be far below the local County tax evaluation of about $1.4

million. Now the decision had been fully made and we were assured that a divine hand was leading and that the future was now determined.

Much discussion revolved around the name of the new Institute. The name, Hartland, they agreed, should be retained. At this meeting the official name was voted: Hartland Institute of Health and Education.

Having a great desire to work in harmony with denominational leadership, Hal Mayer and I visited North American Division, Columbia Union and Potomac Conference leaders. We explained our plans with the Executive Director of the North American Division Board of Higher Education. We were disappointed in his response. He urged us not to go ahead with the project, fearing it would hurt enrollment at Columbia Union College. We explained that the new college would attract a different student from those enrolling at Columbia Union College.

Our visit with Elder Wally Coe, the Columbia Union President, later to be a Vice-President of the General Conference, proved much more favorable. He shared genuine interest in the project and prayed for its success. The President of the Potomac Conference was very straightforward with us. He told us frankly that he wished that we had chosen another Conference in which to locate Hartland, but we were convinced that God had led us to Virginia. Though disappointed with the response, we were not discouraged, and determined to work with the brethren in the Conference wherever possible.

# 4  The Negotiations

*So Hanameel mine uncle's son came to me in the court of the prison according to the word of the Lord, and said unto me, Buy my field, I pray thee, that is in Anathoth, which is in the country of Benjamin: for the right of inheritance is thine, and the redemption is thine; buy it for thyself. Then I knew that this was the word of the Lord.*
— Jeremiah 32:8

HEN I first visited Hartland Hall Plantation in October of 1982 my response was mixed. It was located in a beautiful rural area in the Piedmont Valley of Virginia, with rolling countryside surrounded by farm land which was given over largely to the production of corn, soy beans, winter wheat, and livestock enterprises, mostly beef cattle—yet the rundown condition of the property made it quite unattractive. No doubt that was, in God's providence, reducing the price, something that was most necessary. The property was involved in litigation and was offered for sale by the Madison County Court as a means of settling the case. It had been arranged for us to dialogue with the court-appointed attorneys, Lloyd Sullenberger from Orange and Martin McGettrick from Madison, the latter being the county in which Hartland Hall Plantation is located. Attorney Sullenberger, who was later to become the Madison County judge, was clearly the stronger and more influential of the two attorneys.

After surveying the property and searching out the location of the various homes on the property, the decision was made that we should not make an offer for the full eleven hundred and ninety-two acres. This proposal had first been suggested by Dr. Raymond Moore. It was more land than we needed and certainly it required much more cash than we were prepared to consider. Some months earlier, some friends of the enterprise; Dr. Raymond Moore, Mr. Don Yohe, Dr. Ed Latimer, and Mr. O. D. McKee, had visited the property with Hal and Betsy Mayer. At that time Dr. Moore suggested that we consider making an offer on a portion of the Hartland Hall Plantation. Now we had adopted this counsel.

One hundred and eighty-seven acres of the property lay on the southern side of County Road 614. We decided not to make an offer for that section of the property. We determined that of the fourteen homes, ten of them as well as the mansion were within relatively accessible distance of each other in the northeastern corner of the property. We estimated that approximately five hundred acres would be satisfactory to provide what was needed for Hartland's future work with ample room for expansion.

After a season of prayer, we met with Attorneys Sullenberger and McGettrick; shortly into the dialogue I asked the question, "Would you consider an offer for the northeastern five hundred acres of the property?" There was a pause. Sullenberger looked at McGettrick and eventually said, "Well, only last week we discussed the possibility of selling the property in two or three lots." Realizing that the door to divide was opening, I pressed forward asking, "How much would you require for the five hundred northeastern acres?" Sullenberger responded, "Well, it is up to you to make an offer." I pointed out that we were not experienced in negotiating with courts. We knew how to negotiate with real estate agents and private owners, but they would have to give us some direction on the likely acceptance price. Sullenberger answered that the five hundred acres, though less than half the acreage of the property, nevertheless included most of the buildings, making it more valuable than the rest of the property.

When the Madison County Court was ready to advertise the property for sale, a number of real estate agents in the region had been asked to evaluate it. In spite of its rundown condition the highest evaluation was $3.8 million dollars, the lowest was $2.4 million. The variation in the estimates was strong evidence of the difficulty in making a judgment on such a property, in light of its rundown condition and the loss of many of the assets that had been stolen by the previous owner. Eventually the court chose a Charlottesville real estate agent, Frank Hardy, who had evaluated the land at $2.6 million, to list the property. The court set the asking price for the property at $2.5 million and listed this price on all of the brochures concerning the sale. However, land was exceptionally difficult to sell in the early 1980s. Some who can remember back that far will recall that interest rates were between eighteen and twenty percent per annum or more, and it was very difficult to move large properties under those circumstances. After very few prospective buyers showed an interest in the property, and with no serious offers received, the court decided, less than two months before we expressed an interest in the property, to reduce the selling price to $1,950,000. It seemed to us that God had more ways than one to "raise funds" to cover the cost to start this important work. This was a $550,000 savings. As we were buying about half of the property, this translated into a reduction of about $250,000 for the portion of the property in which we were interested. This was two hundred and fifty thousand God would not have to help us raise.

We waited for Attorney Sullenberger's response regarding how much the five hundred acres would be worth. Finally he responded, "Well, we would need to get $900,000 to a million out of that section." Of course, when he made that statement we immediately thought $900,000, not one million. As stated in the previous chapter, it was eventually decided to offer $750,000 dollars. The unofficial response from Attorneys Sullenberger and McGettrick to that offer was, "The offer is too low to take to the court. Why don't you try $850,000?" We had found that there was a little negotiation which we could make with the court and we resubmitted our offer for $850,000. We were soon to realize that the two largest ponds at the back of the property, one of fifteen acres and the other six acres, would not be part of the property, and we desired to have those features on our property.

A meeting of the Board of Directors by conference call led to a unanimous decision to negotiate for the additional land. I contacted Dr. John Hart, the former owner of the property, who had been helpful in the earlier negotiations. He was asked if he could help reduce the asking price, now $940,000. I suggested that the full 575 acres be made available to us for $900,000. Two days later Doctor Hart responded. He had been in contact with Milligan College, the previous owner (and largest litigant in the court case), and with the Court, and reported that the Court had said, "Tell them to make their offer." That sounded promising, and with the Lord's blessing the offer was accepted.

We sought one further concession. When board members reviewed the $900,000 purchase price, they did not know how they could raise such a large amount of money. There seemed but one hope—to negotiate a significant down payment and then to agree upon a quarterly payment schedule. This too, was a requested exception from the Court's stated conditions of a cash sale.

In February of 1983, I conducted a series of meetings in Woodbury and Smithville, Tennessee. Though it was a five-hour drive from Johnson City, I decided to meet there with Elder Milo Sawvel, our Development Director, and Hal Mayer, and to visit Dr. and Mrs. Hart and the leaders of Milligan College. Increasingly it appeared to us that the Court was seeking to please the leaders of Milligan College more than the other litigants involved in the case. This put them in "the driving seat" regarding the proposed sale.

We met the President of Milligan College, Dr. Marshall Leggett, and the College's Development Director, Pastor Marshall. They offered to accept a down payment and a twenty-year mortgage which they believed Milligan College would hold for us. Later their Board agreed. This was a big breakthrough for us. We felt it unreasonable for us to raise the whole purchase price, when so many other things would need financial attention during the start-up phase. The college would accept a down payment of $275,000, with the rest to be paid over the next twenty years at a rate of interest fixed at ten percent. They also agreed that, should we finalize the payment before the twenty years, there would be no prepayment penalty. When we calculated the details we found that compared to the current rate of twelve and one-third percent interest, we would be saving about $100,000 over a twenty-year period. Every step of the negotiating God had blessed. The impossible became a reality. If we had ever doubted the Lord's leadership, it was now impossible to do so.

Brother Hal Mayer and I, the only representatives of the interim board of directors, along with real estate agent Art Palmer, were present at the Madison Court to observe the hearing upon our offer. The presiding judge, Judge Berry, was meticulous in his deliberations. Because of the "checkered history" of the property and the fraudulent activities associated with the dealings of the previous contract "owner," every effort was made to check out our credibility. For example, it was learned that a number of those who were associated with and supporting this project had been staff members at Weimar Institute in Placer County, California. Unbeknown to us, the court had checked Placer County's evaluation of Weimar College and, by the grace of God, they had received a very favorable report. That proved to be a great help in the judge's decision. Brother Mayer and I were called to give testimony. The Judge plied us with many pointed questions which we answered to his apparent satisfaction. The judge was determined to ensure, as far as possible, that there would not be a repetition of the problems which had occurred with the previous "owner." Suddenly, almost anticlimactically, the judge approved our offer. Judge Berry declared, "I believe this is in the interests of all parties" when making judgment in our favor.

Now in the negotiations conducted before the court hearings, we set down two conditions with the attorneys. They were reluctant to agree with these conditions but we told them we would have no interest whatsoever in the property unless these conditions were met: (1) that the sale would be subject to the voting of a variance by Madison County permitting us to operate a college on the property; (2) that the Madison County

Board of Supervisors would also grant permission to operate a health center on the property. Those clauses were added to the agreement and therefore the agreement would become binding only when the County voted favorably upon our application for a special use permit to fulfill these two conditions.

There were other issues requiring much negotiating and dialogue. These issues included traffic load, number of people on campus, water and sewage, fire and police protection, hospital facilities, and taxes. All were discussed with the county leaders and resolved to their satisfaction and ours.

# 5

# The Financing

*The children of Israel brought a willing offering unto the LORD, every man and woman, whose heart made them willing to bring for all manner of work, which the LORD had commanded to be made by the hand of Moses.* —Exodus 35:29

OD had already given us the earnest of His blessing when Brother O. D. McKee promised $150,000 towards the start-up costs of the new Institute. We had seen God's wonderful leading, step by step, through many difficulties, and we had placed our trust fully in Him. However, we had agreed to Milligan College's requirement of a down payment of $275,000 by July 1, 1983. $45,000 had already been placed in escrow with the Madison County Court twenty days before the court hearing and a further $45,000 was required to be placed with the court within twenty days of the favorable outcome. Few people could offer large donations, and many of the donations which came, as continues to be the case, were one hundred dollars or less. Praise God for these regular donors. However, it stood to reason that there needed to be many contributors to reach the additional $185,000 still outstanding. Elder Milo Sawvel, the former associate director of the Temperance Department of the General Conference of Seventh-day Adventists, did an active and noble work in seeking out donations from a wide spectrum of men and women whom he encouraged to support the new institute.

Once the court had ruled in our favor on the purchase of the property, there were many other issues to negotiate. The major one, besides financing, was to obtain the variances we needed from the county so that we could operate a college and a health facility. We spent considerable time with Steve Utz, the county administrator, and David Jones, the chairman of the Madison County Planning Commission who was later to become the chairman of the Board of Supervisors for the county. We discussed many issues with them. They asked about education of the children of the staff. We assured these county leaders that we would be placing no increased financial responsibility upon the county school system, as our children would be educated at Hartland. This assurance met their approval.

The county leaders were deeply concerned about the loss of revenue from such a sizeable property because of our tax-free status. Madison County is relatively large in area but has a very small population. At that time it had only a little in excess of ten thousand residents in the whole county. Realistically, they needed income from a property of the size we proposed to purchase. We eventually came to an agreement that to protect our tax-exempt status we would not pay any taxes, but would make a contribution every year in lieu of taxes, which we continue to do. Both leaders seemed favorable to our project and proposal, and to the variances we were seeking. However, we were to find that the process would be more difficult and would take longer than we had anticipated. The biggest immediate hurdle we faced was to accumulate the second $45,000, representing five percent of the total purchase price of the property, within twenty days of the court's decision in our favor. Once again Elder Sawvel took charge of this endeavor. The McKees had sent $25,000 toward the second payment, but we needed to raise another $20,000 in twenty days—donations totaling $1,000 per day. Elder Sawvel worked with great vigor and energy.

On the Thursday before the second payment of $45,000 was due, I received a call from Elder Sawvel, who was in the field seeking donations from as many individuals as he knew. His call was not encouraging—he told me that he was still at least $7,000 short of the $45,000. He had called to ask if I knew of any other persons who could be approached. Unfortunately I knew of no one else—I had given him all the names I thought might have the slightest interest in helping the project. Very seriously we prayed together on the phone asking God to bless and to guide us and to bring the necessary funds. We reminded the Lord that He had brought us this far and we believed that He would carry us through. It was another of the many moments in which we had to exercise faith. Yet even I was not ready for the rapid answer to our prayers. Within a couple of hours Elder Sawvel was back to me on the telephone. The animation of his voice told me that the Lord had wonderfully answered our prayers, and so He had.

Before his initial call to me, Elder Sawvel had called his home asking his wife, Marian, if any donations had come in that day. She said a few had come in and she read them out. They varied between ten dollars and one hundred dollars, none of which significantly altered the need for over seven thousand dollars. Yet we were very grateful to the donors. God blesses with little as He blesses with much. Still, we needed some major donations among the smaller ones, grateful though we were for them. No doubt prompted by the Holy Spirit, Elder Sawvel telephoned his wife, Marian, again and asked her to review carefully the checks which she had received that morning. Dutifully she did so, reading off the donations until she came to the ten-dollar check and was about to proceed when she said, "No, it's not ten dollars, it's ten thousand dollars!" This check had been sent from Dr. Everett Kuester, a physician in Georgia, whom at that time we did not know. He expressed his interest in the project and his pleasure to give a "small" donation to help toward the establishment of the institution. Of course my joy knew no bounds. Once again our blessed Lord had met our need, reaffirming His divine approval of the project. Duly the $45,000 was sent to escrow, and now we were left with two final hurdles to surmount: (1) to obtain a zoning variance to operate a college and a health center, and (2) to raise an additional $185,000, making up the $275,000 down payment necessary to take possession of the property on July 1.

As we had not found it easy to obtain the first $90,000, half before the court's decision and half afterward, we knew that it would be a very difficult task. But again our faith in the Lord had been strengthened. The McKees promised to send the other $105,000 from their initial pledge of $150,000. That still left us with eighty thousand dollars to raise in a little over two months. To this day I have no true picture of the sources from which all that eighty thousand dollars came. But one thing I do know, by the miracle of God's blessings we were able to deposit the required amount with Milligan College by July 1. What a friend we have in Jesus! He has never failed us nor forsaken us.

In the meantime there was still pending the necessary approval of variances for us to operate the college and the health center. Time was running out. Quite a number of the new staff members had tendered their resignation notices to Weimar Institute so that in fairness to Weimar, that institution could be searching for replacements for various positions. Some were leaving employment responsibilities in other regions of the United States. But not one wavered, despite the fact that we did not have as yet full assurance that the institution would definitely go forward on July 1.

By the beginning of April, 1983, we were in a position to lodge our application for the needed variances. After due consideration the Madison County Planning Committee of twelve members recommended to the Board of Supervisors that there be a one-month extension before a decision be made so that further input from the community could be solicited. At that time we had no idea what led to this extension of time. We had, with the realtor, visited most of the home owners within a reasonable range of the Hartland Hall Plantation, seeking to explain the nature of the college we would be operating, and also to seek their support and to answer any questions that they might have had in their minds. We were happy with the response we received from the property owners and felt that none of them was likely to oppose our application for use permits. Thus I was puzzled by the delay in finalizing our application. This meant that when the decision was made it would be less than two months before the hoped-for occupancy, July 1.

As we reasoned together, however, we saw so many providential leadings of the Lord that we were convinced that the final decision would be favorable. None of those who pledged themselves to be part of the initial Hartland staff wavered under the uncertainty of this delay. At the May session of the Madison County meeting of the Board, the Planning Commission unanimously voted to accept the proposal which we had made, and this decision was ratified by the Board of Supervisors. Little did we know, however, what had caused the delay and what had led to the unanimous vote in favor of our proposal.

It was not until several months after Hartland Institute had commenced that we learned what had been going on behind the scenes within the Planning Commission, and what later led to the unanimous decision in favor of our proposal. We learned of this turmoil only when we were invited to an interview at the local Orange radio station. Before the interview, the lady who was to conduct the interview asked how much we knew about the opposition engendered by our proposal. We said we had not heard the least word about it. Then she explained, "The planning commissioner who lived closest to Hartland Hall Plantation had greatly opposed our application. He visited the other planning commissioners, urging them to vote against the proposal. The last thing he wanted close to where he lived was a college community." He had conjured up in his mind the traditional college situation with the use of alcohol, drugs, partying and other aspects of college life which are common disturbances to a community. Also, Hartland's proposal called for a potential population of four hundred, made up of staff families, students and health guests. This commissioner was afraid that this section of the county would become overpopulated! It was his opposition which led the planning commission in April of 1983 to vote a one-month extension before reaching its final decision.

Once again God intervened. During the one-month delay, apparently without prior notification, the Virginia Correctional Authority sent representatives into Madison County seeking a location for a new State prison.

In their quest they visited Hartland Hall Plantation and examined it as a possible location for the proposed new prison. Soon word reached the planning commissioners, including the commissioner who was opposing our application. With lightening swiftness he reversed his opposition to our proposal. We understand that he contacted all the commissioners anew, urging them now to vote for our proposal, fearing any thought of having a prison built within close proximity to his own property. We were told he uttered the words, "Thank the Lord for the Seventh-day Adventists!" Our thoughts were, "Thank you Lord for Your intervention." Eventually a new prison was built, not in Madison County, but in Culpeper County, about six miles from where Hartland Institute is located. God had wrought on our behalf once more.

At the May meeting of the Planning Commission and Board of Supervisors there was only one voice of dissent, and that was from one of the month-by-month renters living on the property. No doubt he desired to stay in the home and opposed the special-use permit, knowing full well that he would receive one month's notification when the Board of Supervisors had agreed to the usage variance.

Now everything was ready for the thrilling task of raising up another institution to the glory of God, for the hastening of His coming, for the training of young people and the healing of the sick.

Dick Mayer of the Laurel Nursing Center, Hamburg, Pennsylvania, witnessed the rewarding moment with his son Hal and real estate agent, Art Palmer, when on July 1, 1983, the final settlement on the five hundred seventy-five acres of the Hartland Hall Plantation was sealed for the newly incorporated Hartland Institute of Health and Education. Dick and his wife, the late Laurena, had constantly encouraged and supported the task force's efforts to commence Hartland Institute. It had been six months, from the January 1 meeting of the Advisory Committee held in Burnt Mills Church where the decision was taken to purchase Hartland Hall Plantation, to the final settlement upon the property. It had been just over eleven months since the 122 brethren and sisters had gathered at Blue Mountain Academy in Pennsylvania to express their support for the establishment of such an institution on the East Coast of the United States. Dick and Laurena Mayer, however, offered more than moral support. They donated $80,000 over a period of time to underwrite the project to assure its success. How great is our God!

Later, in the providence of God we were able to retire the mortgage in less than nine and one-half years. However, a number of years before that, Brother Richard Becker generously took over the debt so that we could complete the payment to Milligan College. Brother Becker reduced the interest rate from ten to six percent, saving much precious financial resources. Adding to his wonderful contribution he donated the final $50,000 of the debt. God has greatly blessed Hartland with dedicated supporters.

# 6  The Property

*I will raise up agents who will carry out My will to prepare a people to stand before Me in the time of the end. In many places that before this ought to have been provided with sanitariums and schools, I will establish My institutions, and these institutions will become educational centers for the training of workers.*
—*Testimonies for the Church*, Vol. 7, pp. 101, 102

HARTLAND Hall Plantation combined together two adjacent properties known as Lovell and Oakland. These two properties, we were told, had been land grants from King George III of England in the eighteenth century. We were also told that both properties had been worked by slaves. There is a small graveyard on the property of Hartland Institute. It is believed that slaves were buried there. In earlier times American Indians had either lived or at least hunted on the property because, especially during the earlier years of Hartland Institute, quite a number of the stone spearheads commonly used by the Indians were found on the property. Further, it is known that the Civil War passed over the property. The Battle of Cedar Mountain, one well-known battle of the Civil War, took place about five miles from Hartland. During the war the northern army lay one winter in Culpeper, twelve miles north of Hartland, and the southern army in Orange, eight miles south of Hartland. A significant number of both northern and southern bullets and other artifacts have been found on the property. It is easy to differentiate the bullets because the southern have two rings and the northern bullets, three rings. Whether, in fact, any actual fighting took place on the property is doubtful.

The Hartland property is located in the Piedmont Valley east of the Blue Ridge Mountains in very serene and gracious surroundings, divided between sparsely populated residential areas, farm land and forests. Probably every animal and bird life that is seen in the region has been sighted on the Hartland property. There have been three sightings of black bear on the property although most of the bears are located in the more elevated western part of the county. There have been occasional sightings of bald eagles, one of which I saw several years ago.

Eventually the property was purchased by Mr. Smith, the wealthy vice-president of a tobacco company. In 1918 he began the building of the beautiful mansion that graces this property. It is said that Mr. Smith decided to build it for his fiancée who came from New York City. We have been told by descendants of the Smith family that the fiancée absolutely refused to leave the bright lights of New York City for the serenity of rural Virginia. The mansion took five years to build, being completed in 1923. The magnificent sandstone pillars located at what is really the front of the mansion were brought to the property by mule carts from Rapidan railway station three and one-half miles away. The mansion, which consists of a full basement with walls fifteen inches thick and originally two stories, cost $1,050,000—a huge price in that period. We understand that, tragically, Mr. Smith suffered a fatal heart attack on the property when the mansion was almost completed. He never lived there to reap the benefits of his labors.

A nephew and his family moved to the property in 1923 and lived there until 1955. All his children grew up there and when Hartland took possession of the mansion one of the doors on the second floor showed the height of the children at the various ages of their lives. Shortly after we had taken possession of the property, descendants of the Smith family requested that they be able to take that door because of its sentimental value to the family and replace it with another and of course we agreed. Even today occasionally members of the Smith family will pass by to show their descendants the mansion where their forebears grew up and lived.

In 1955 the property was purchased by Dr. John Hart and his wife, Pearl. The Harts were from Tennessee. Dr. Hart had been educated at Milligan College, a college of the Christian Church which also served the youth of the Church of Christ. He was later to become a very important board member of Milligan College and a great benefactor of his alma mater. The young ladies' dormitory at Milligan College is called Hart Hall because of the generosity of the Hart family. Also, in the corridor of the administrative building are two ancient chairs. The plaque above the chairs states that those chairs were donated by Dr. and Mrs. John Hart and were chairs that once belonged to Martin Luther. Dr. Hart was a great collector of antiques from around the world.

By profession he was an educator and had served as the superintendent of schools in a North Carolina county. When he purchased the property in 1955 he renamed it after himself—Hartland Hall Plantation. He became well known in the community and was a member of the

Christian Church. He added quite a number of homes to the property, including four old log homes, all of which he purchased from other parts of Virginia. One, now called log manor, is a rare three-story log home. He purchased these old log homes cheaply and then had each of the logs carefully marked for reassembly on the property. He often said that the three-story log manor had been erected in three counties. Indeed it had been at only two locations, including its present location on Hartland campus, but there had been a change of county boundaries while it occupied its first location. Thus it had been within the boundaries of two different counties. Dr. Hart was known for driving hard bargains and building homes frugally. The homes also had deteriorated during the seven years after the Harts left the property. This led to the need for much improvement of the homes which were present when we first arrived at Hartland Hall Plantation.

Dr. and Mrs. Hart decided in 1977 to retire to Johnson City, Tennessee, where they lived until their deaths. Pearl, who was about four years older than Dr. Hart, died at eighty-nine years of age early in 1985; Dr. Hart died in July of 1985 in a retirement center in Johnson City at the age of eighty-five. He was exceedingly happy that a college was being established at his former home. An educator himself, he had decided to offer the property as a gift to anyone who would operate a college on the property. More than five years passed before we heard about the property. Dr. Hart told me that in desperation he offered the property to the Roman Catholics, but even they showed no interest in establishing an educational facility there. I have often thought that it was at that very time that Columbia Union College was investigating the possibility of obtaining a new location in the country. He would have gladly donated the property free of charge to the Seventh-day Adventists. However, no one was aware of it. In the end Dr. Hart donated the property to his alma mater, Milligan College, for it to realize the profit from its sale.

Eventually a professed buyer came forward, claiming the name of Mr. Fine. There are many who doubt that was his real name. Mr. Fine asked to check out the property with Dr. Hart. He claimed to be a mining magnate and during the course of the tour of the property Mr. Fine asked to make a phone call in the presence of Dr. Hart. He spoke as if he were speaking to one of his managers, making statements such as, "Well, if you need to, run in another mile of railway line . . ." Dr. Hart was convinced that he was "a con-man." He made this clear to the then president of Milligan College, Dr. Johnson. Yet in spite of Dr. Hart's warning, the Milligan College Board "sold" the property to Mr. Fine with no down payment! In the years that Mr. Fine was associated with the property he paid not one cent to Milligan College. He plundered all the valuables he could find, including the machinery of the silos and other valuable pieces of equipment. He had incurred over $400,000 of debt owed to businesses within the region when the Madison County Court seized the property. But just as law enforcement officers were moving in on him, Mr. Fine disappeared. It was believed by some that he escaped to Brazil. At least one person in the community claimed that he had seen Mr. Fine back in the region, but when he addressed him as "Mr. Fine" there was no response or acknowledgment. Whatever happened, Mr. Fine has paid no debt to society for his criminal activities.

Immediately the court took over the disposition of the property. Many liens were made against it from businesses defrauded by Mr. Fine. However, the court, after two deliberations, ruled that no liens could be held against the property because the fraudulent acts were those of Mr. Fine, not of the property nor of the former owner of the property, Milligan College. The court further ruled that the property would be placed on the market under the condition that never could these old liens be lodged against the new owner. That was very reassuring to us as we were negotiating for the purchase of the property. However, the scandal spread far and wide and was especially intensely dialogued in the Madison, Culpeper and Orange newspapers as well as the local Orange radio station. The property certainly became well-known in the area, but not for noble reasons.

Dr. Hart worked very closely with us and on a number of occasions came to revisit the property. He and his wife spent some time in the wellness program, as their health was rapidly deteriorating. One special moment which I remember well occurred when I was showing some visitors over the mansion. Dr. and Mrs. Hart were visiting at the time and as I was walking down the upstairs hall, Pearl Hart came out of the room where she was staying. I introduced the visitors to her and immediately she took over telling them all sorts of interesting facets about the mansion. It was a poignant moment for me as she seemed to regress to an earlier time when she was the hostess of that mansion. She would pass away only a few months later.

Dr. Hart gave to us a number of antiques for the institution. Included were the furnishings for one of the second-floor rooms which in the early days of Hartland Wellness Center we used for health center guests. He was also particularly anxious for us to purchase the one hundred and eighty-seven acres on the southern side of County Route 614. We told him we would love to have that piece of property, but at twelve hundred dollars an acre, which was the price at that time, there was no way, in view of the other financial needs we had, that we could justify such a purchase. He then negotiated with Milligan College to have the property sold to us for six hundred dollars an acre. But that was still significantly more than $100,000.

Again I told Dr. Hart that while I appreciated his efforts, we could not consider the purchase of that part of the property. He was persistent, however. He told me that he had decided to send fifty thousand dollars worth of bonds which would mature between 1996 and 2006. Of course, they would not be of help until they were cashed. Dr. Hart said they were probably worth about two-thirds of fifty thousand dollars at that time. Maybe we could realize about thirty thousand dollars if we could find a purchaser for these bonds. As we will see, that actually took place, although tragic circumstances would arise which left us to find other ways to pay off almost eighty thousand dollars on that property. We have never regretted purchasing the one hundred and eighty-seven acres south of County Route 614. It has been a great protection against potentially undesirable neighbors moving into that part of the property. Thus today Hartland Institute comprises seven hundred sixty-one acres, four acres having been donated to Madison County to widen the road past Hartland Institute. I believe today that Hartland Institute property is truly sacred and holy ground.

# 7 The Open Houses

*While we are not to seek to wrest property from any man, yet when advantages are offered, we should be wide awake to see the advantage, that we may make plans for the upbuilding of the work. And when we have done this we should exert every energy to secure the freewill offerings of God's people for the support of these new plants.* —*Testimonies for the Church*, Vol. 9, p. 272

"YOU Adventists stole this property!" exclaimed Dr. John Hart, former owner of Hartland Hall Plantation. He was alluding to the very low price we had negotiated for the property. I assured him that Hartland was divinely appointed and that God had led each step. Dr. Hart responded, "There's no people I'd rather have occupy this property than the Adventists."

The court had given permission for an open house prior to the final purchase. However they forbade any general announcements in the community because there had been no final settlements. The guests would have to be alerted by private invitation. We had to send these invitations to leaders and church friends in the community. Dr. Hart and his wife Pearl had accepted the invitation to attend this first of two Open Houses, May 22, 1983. Retired in Johnson City, Tennessee, the Harts had lived at Hartland for twenty-one and a half years. Dr. Hart had been delighted when he heard of our interest in the property for the establishment of a college and health center. He was delighted to be with us for this open house.

Dr. Warren Peters and I flew from the West Coast for the special event. In the morning, the Board of Directors had met. A heavy morning rain continued until two o'clock in the afternoon, when the open house was to begin, and then abruptly stopped. We had no doubt that God had blessed us once more, because in the morning we had prayed earnestly for the rain to cease during the open house. Despite the rain, over four hundred guests attended the open house. The event was well organized by Elder Milo Sawvel. Volunteers from Orange and Culpeper Seventh-day Adventist Churches had helped cut the grass and erect a tent and place chairs, loaned by the Potomac Conference of Seventh-day Adventists.

We were greatly privileged to have Moisés Parker to be the guest soloist. I first met Moisés, a Cuban, when he flew from Havana to Mexico City and then to Kingston, Jamaica, to be associated with West Indies College. Moisés is a world-class tenor. A Jamaican patron sponsored him to study further in Munich, Germany, and later he sang with many of the famous European orchestras as a guest tenor. He went on to win the Verdi International contest in Italy and the Barcelona International in Spain. There is no question he was one of the greatest black tenors in the world. When I was president of Columbia Union College he became a voice teacher at the college. On this occasion he was visiting back in the United States and graciously accepted my invitation to sing at this open house. Without accompaniment, he thrilled the attendees with his rendition of the Lord's Prayer. This open house created much interest for the soon-to-be-established institution.

Present were representatives from the General Conference, Columbia Union Conference, and Potomac Conference of Seventh-day Adventists. Also present were representatives of U. S. Senator John Warner and U. S. Representative Robinson. Virginia delegate George Baird was also present. Local government was well represented by Steve Utz, County Administrator, David Jones, Chairman of the Planning Commission and other leaders. The local church community, as well as many from the Washington, D.C. area came for the occasion. The strongest speech was delivered by Dr. Hart himself, whose enthusiasm was infectious. "I'm eighty-four years of age," he began, "and this is the best day of my life! Praise the Lord!"

A second open house was held on a Sunday in November. This time the public announcements brought another sizeable group to witness God's mighty work. There were refreshments, fellowship, and tours of the mansion. People envisioned what Hartland could become under God's leadership. The property, once said to have been worked by slaves, was now dedicated to the freedom that Christ alone can provide.

My last visit with Dr. Hart was after the death of his wife, Pearl. He was grieving greatly and was mainly confined to his bed. Yet he still had sufficient strength and enthusiasm to tell me he wished he could live to see the mature development of Hartland Institute. He was truly a unique man. I believe if he were still alive he would greatly have rejoiced in God's providences and leadings in the further development of the institution.

# 8 The Arrival

*Moses my servant is dead; now therefore arise, go over this Jordan, thou, and all this people, unto the land which I do give to them, even to the children of Israel.* —Joshua 1:2

THE first staff began to arrive on the property on Independence Day, July 4, 1983. Among those who arrived that day were the Mayers, the Blums and the Goleys. My wife Cheryl and I, together with our infant adopted son Nigel, did not arrive until the twenty-sixth of July, despite our desire to be there right from the beginning. It had all to do with the fact that the adoption of our son had not been finalized and we could not leave California until that had taken place.

Our departure from Weimar Institute was delayed a little longer because I had accepted the invitation to preach the following weekend at a retreat by a lake in northern California. Before we left for our new home in Virginia, after five happy years in California, a hired semitrailer driven by Brother Hal Mayer's brother, Richard, collected our furnishings, together with the furnishings of others who were to be a part of the pioneer staff at Hartland. Soon we bade farewell to our friends at Weimar Institute and other parts of California and were driving to meet our new challenge. I had never before traveled across the United States by road, but my wife, Cheryl, had done so when she drove with one of her friends to Weimar several weeks after I had arrived there to plan for the first college year at that institution in 1978. The journey proved to be a very interesting experience, highlighted by a brief visit to Yellowstone National Park and to the Black Hills of South Dakota. During our travel we were somewhat delayed because of a brief sickness which Nigel had developed but, apart from that, the journey went smoothly and we arrived safely on the twenty-sixth of July.

We arrived during daytime and witnessed our colleagues busily engaged in the hard work of reclaiming the campus and beginning to restore it to its full beauty. I felt badly that we could not have helped in those first three weeks, but I witnessed the tremendous will and effort which had already been put into the work. The late Pastor Daniel O'Ffill, a retired pastor, had kindly loaned his Bush Hog, a most valuable implement considering the height of the grass around the campus area. New discoveries were made. For example, we had no idea that there were brick paths leading to the formal garden, but as that area was being cleared, the path, overrun with grass and moss, was now uncovered. It had almost the appearance of an archaeological dig. But cleaning up the property was just a small part of the task. Every building needed much repair and help. It was to take years for us to bring everything to a reasonable level of habitability. The task of leading out in the maintenance was the responsibility of Brother Earl Schoonard. He worked with great dedication with few hands to aid him. Of course, the restoration of the mansion was a huge undertaking, not completed until a number of years later. Thanks to the good leadership of Earl's wife Darlis, the major part of the restoration was completed by May, 1984, in time to receive our first health guest.

As other new staff came there was great rejoicing. Every new face, every new member was counted as a great blessing, for they represented a little more man- and woman-power to help us in the gigantic task. Yet there was great joy in what we were doing. Only those who have been part of a new pioneering adventure will understand the cohesiveness and the cooperation which there is among the eager, energetic, enthusiastic and dedicated pioneers. There was no thought of background training or professionalism. Whatever needed to be done, we were each, according to our abilities, willing to give our all to accomplish. It mattered not whether one was a physician, an educator, a nurse, or a business person, we all did what must be done to prepare the mansion ready for occupancy and for the first college school year, set to begin September 23, 1983.

I will never forget the arrival of many of our medical team. We were in the midst of prayer meeting. We were engaged in prayer and during that season of prayer we had prayed earnestly for the safe arrival of the medical staff. We knew they were expected some time that day. We had not completed our prayer when we heard the happy praises of Linda Ball, Heather Houck, Ronda Potterton, and Dr. and Mrs. Peters and their family, who had come to be part of the initial health team at Hartland Institute. We were soon off our knees and welcoming the newcomers. Again we knelt in prayer with these additional staff as we all thanked God for His protection in bringing these dedicated men and women to serve at Hartland Institute.

# 9

# The Pioneer Staff

*After these things the Lord appointed other seventy also, and sent them two and two before his face into every city and place, whither he himself would come. Therefore said he unto them, The harvest truly is great, but the labourers are few: pray ye therefore the Lord of the harvest, that he would send forth labourers into his harvest. Go your ways: behold, I send you forth as lambs among wolves. Carry neither purse, nor script, nor shoes: and salute no man by the way. And into whatsoever house ye enter, first say, Peace be to this house.*                               —Luke 10:1–5

IMMEDIATELY after graduation exercises at Weimar College, Dr. John Goley, his wife Kathy, and their three-year-old daughter Jennifer, journeyed eastward. John, who had taught for three years in the Health Science Department of Weimar College, had accepted the appointment to be the foundational chairman of the Health Ministries Department at Hartland College.

The Goleys were the first family to arrive at the property. They could not move onto the site, however, because renters had until July 1 to leave. Culpeper Church friends, the Toracs, housed them until July 4, when, with others, they moved onto the property.

Quickly others arrived: The Blums (Dr. Dennis, Carol and daughter Dawn); Dennis was appointed Dean of the college. The Mayers (Hal and Betsy) arrived; Hal was under appointment to be my Assistant, Betsy was appointed to teach in the college and serve in food service. The Schoonards (Earl and Darlis) arrived early. Earl was appointed Director of Plant Development, Darlis to supervise mansion restoration. The Grams (David, Cheryl, Kevin, Lynn and Lori) soon made their way to Hartland. David had accepted appointment to teach in the Bible Department.

The small group of pioneers had to "tame the jungle," the result of seven years of neglect. Pathways were uncovered. The wisteria and other vines which covered areas of the property around the mansion were cut away. The formal gardens on the east side of the mansion would soon be considerably restored.

In late summer, the Hamman family arrived (Gerald, Pam, Sonny, Jennifer, Tamara); Gerald had accepted the role of Food Service Director. The Hammans were followed by Jan Watson, the Dean of Women and Director of Admissions. She had driven with her mother from Auburn, California. The next arrivals were Elder Milo and Marian Sawvel; Milo had accepted the responsibility of Financial Development/Public Relations Director, and Student Outreach Director; Marian was appointed to the business office.

One great setback occurred—the house allocated to the Sawvels had to be dismantled because it was infested by termites! This problem led to considerable hardship for the Sawvels. For many months, including the winter, they huddled in a small trailer and a motor home. Eventually Elsworth McKee donated $20,000 toward the building of the replacement home, overlooking one of Hartland's lovely ponds.

In late August the first of the medical team arrived. Before leaving the west, the team had spent a month at Weimar Institute where they observed the medical program. Dr. Warren Peters had left a prosperous practice in peripheral vascular surgery in Spokane, Washington, to become the Medical Director of Hartland's Health Program. Hartland leadership had become familiar with Warren during the previous two summers when student teams from Weimar worked with him to conduct a health education program in Spokane. His wife, Jeanie, was under appointment to teach at the Canwick Pines Academy, a self-supporting high school near Fredericksburg (presently not operating), where a number of our staff children attended. The Peters had with them their daughter, Adena.

Linda Ball, Heather Houck and Ronda Potterton (now Smith) also arrived with Dr. Peters. Linda, with an R.N. with a health education diploma from Weimar College, came to be the Nursing Coordinator for the live-in program of Hartland's Health Education Center. Heather Houck, a registered dietician from Sonora Hospital in California, had accepted the position of dietician. Ronda, a nurse from Weimar Institute, was chosen to be head nurse at the Capital Health Center in Hyattsville, Maryland, where for five years a health clinic was operated by Hartland Health Center staff.

Late in the year Dr. Everett Kuester arrived. Dr. Kuester was not only an experienced physician, but a competent builder. Dedicated to the work, Dr. Kuester arrived at Hartland several months before his wife could join him.

In January, 1984, the Moseanko family (Rich, Kathie and their three children) arrived; Rich became the Business Manager.

Those first months were stressful. When the euphoria had abated, hard work needed to be accomplished and difficult decisions had to be made. The Administrative Committee sometimes disagreed over the order of priority. Occasionally the administration was viewed as visionary beyond realism.

Some felt that neither educational nor health program should commence until building and renovations were completed. The Administrative Committee, however, was committed to commencing these programs as soon as possible, even though circumstances were not ideal. Further, they recognized that for a ministry which delays the implementation of its programs, support soon evaporates. Administrators believed it was essential to begin the ministries as soon as feasible, even in circumstances less than ideal. An added benefit from an early commencement was that it highlighted a pioneering dimension that strengthened the ministry and bonded the staff and students together in ways that proved beneficial to staff and student morale.

Yet some plans did lack realism. The live-in health program was projected to begin in September. Successive starting dates moved to November, and then January; but the first program was not offered until May of 1984. The workers had underestimated the plumbing, redecoration, and restoration required. Some thought that even May was too early. "I felt we shouldn't have commenced in May, but now I'm so thankful we did!" said Linda Ball. "We have ministered to some whom we would not otherwise have been able to help, both physically and spiritually. If we had waited we would still have felt we were unready."

The college commenced on schedule, September 23, 1984. The thirteen pioneering students soon adapted to their less-than-ideal facilities. As the adage goes, "It is better to have a good teacher in a barn than a poor teacher in a palace."

Pioneering is never easy, but as the workers reflected upon the first year at Hartland, they exclaimed, "What hath God wrought!" There were discouragements, uncertainty, disagreements, but all as seen through the limitations of human weakness, not through any limitations of God. Frequently we reflected upon the journey of Israel to the Promised Land. How often the Israelites exhibited faithlessness and selfishness, and we too had fallen prey to the same sins. My prayer today is that humanity will not continue to hinder Divinity.

# 10     The Sacrifice

*I beseech you therefore, brethren, by the mercies of God, that ye present your bodies a living sacrifice, holy, acceptable unto God, which is your reasonable service. And be not conformed to this world: but be ye transformed by the renewing of your mind, that ye may prove what is that good, and acceptable, and perfect, will of God.*       —Romans 12:1, 2

NOTHING worthwhile for the Lord will ever be established without dedicated sacrifice by the pioneers. It was faith and trust in the Lord, not promise of remuneration, which led the initial staff to accept the invitation to serve at Hartland. I am thankful for the present staff and for their willingness to sacrifice. However, in the initial stages of a project the sacrifices, of necessity, were much greater. They came with no assurance of any remuneration. For several months all we could offer was a stipend of twenty-five dollars per worker per month, a roof over their heads, and a little food on a plate, with no other financial benefit whatsoever. No doubt a few of the staff had a little money in reserve which they could depend upon, but others, especially those who had served at Weimar, had no significant savings. They were depending upon what they had brought with them in their refrigerators and in their freezers. However, God blessed in many ways. There were folk from the Culpeper Church who donated food from their gardens. Irene Torac and Brother Borm from the Culpeper Church brought much produce for the struggling pioneers. We were able for some time to obtain certain food items suitable for our diet from the food bank in Richmond.

I will never forget the kindness of Brother Richard Mayer, who at the conclusion of the Kutztown County Fair not far from where he lived in Pennsylvania, asked the food venders if they would donate the leftover food to this new project. Many kindly did. Now, of course, some of the food was not the kind of food that we would eat. A considerable amount of it was flesh food. However, Brother Mayer was willing to exchange this for vegetarian alternatives and use the food in his nursing home. This was a great blessing to the staff. God made sure that no one was without food. Eventually we were able to vote staff members a fifty dollars per month stipend (a one hundred percent increase) and to provide small "food allowances" for each member of the family. The food allowance was eighty dollars a month for each individual thirteen years of age and over, sixty dollars a month for children seven to twelve, and forty dollars a month for children six and under. We all knew that staff could not survive for long on such meager finances. There was much prayer for God to protect the cars from damage or mechanical failures, for we understood that very few families were in a position to pay for repairs and maintenance of their vehicles. Certainly God blessed this sacrifice of the staff. But this was only one area of sacrifice. All accepted the sacrificial allowance and, despite hardship, none of the staff chose to leave during the first year.

Great efforts were required to make the grounds presentable. However, as indicated earlier, Elder Daniel O'Ffill's generous loan of his Bush Hog allowed David Grams and his ground crew to begin to develop the lawn in front of the entrance to the mansion and around it.

Yet despite this dedication, large bills accumulated monthly. Despite the most frugal use of funds, the situation was extremely tight. In the early months of Hartland, without a business manager, accounting was difficult. Upon his arrival, however, business officer Rich Moseanko implemented sound fiscal policies.

Regular bills needed to be kept current. The quarterly debt reduction payment upon the property was in excess of $18,000. Electricity bills sometimes soared around $2,000 monthly and telephone bills averaged around $1,100 per month. Salaries, allowances and travel expenses exceeded $5,000 per month. There was the huge need for repairs, maintenance, and new construction. These costs were prohibitive to the small, infant institution. However, there were contributors who lovingly supported by sending regular monthly donations. These regular donors, as today, formed the backbone of the rapidly expanding ministry of Hartland Institute.

The needs increased, yet the internal sources of income were small. Later there were fees from our few college students and a small income from the Capital Health Center after it began operating in Hyattsville. Still later there was a beginning income from the live-in program of the Hartland Health Center, as well as some outpatient income. Altogether these sources could not begin to cover the large expenses which accumulated daily. At that moment in the history of Hartland we had no funds available for the ministry we dearly desired to undertake. We could hardly fund the minimal costs which were accruing.

The old buildings, when put under stress from staff and student traffic, presented challenges that caused service interruptions. For example it would seem that the water pipes were of poor quality, for they broke in a number of places resulting in disruption of water service until the leak was located and necessary repairs made. Yet the staff members took all these difficulties in their stride, pressing forward to the goals God had set before us.

Many of the homes were left in such a state by the departing itinerant renters that it was obvious much work had to be accomplished before those to whom they had been assigned could actually dwell in them. Thus in the beginning of Hartland Institute's ministry there were seven families living in log manor, each one assigned one room. One at a time, as homes were made habitable, the families departed for more spacious accommodations. Yet, amazingly, I do not remember one word of anger, one complaint or one discontented word. I am convinced that pioneering brings out the best in God's people.

But other sacrifices were made. For example, on the western side of the campus, including the mansion and nearby homes, there was almost no water supply. There was a well-house between the mansion and the first home but it supplied only a trickle of water. It took us several months to discover that the water supply which gave adequate service to the eastern side of the campus, was able to supply the western side also. All it took was the opening of a valve. But for those months before this discovery, those on the western side had no alternative but to bathe and do their washing at the homes of those who lived on the eastern side of the campus. Of course, those who were on the eastern side were only too happy to open their homes for those who had need. It was a time of great working together and cooperation, where the needs of one were gladly served by the resources of others.

When school was about to commence, we faced the problem of where the students would be accommodated. It was decided that the young men would be accommodated in the mansion, including the basement—hardly a desirable place to live. For a number of years that area was home to the young men. The basement dorm-home was known as "the dungeon." There was no single building suitable for the young ladies, thus it was decided that they would be accommodated in staff homes. We had two of the young ladies in our home who proved a blessing to us. They were true Christian young ladies. Others were accommodated in other workers' homes.

Perhaps the most difficult and undesirable task which I fulfilled in those early days came when, because of the previous renters, the septic tank serving our home was blocked with objects which should never have been flushed down a toilet. We had to empty the septic tank. I had the volunteer help of Brother Hal Mayer who graciously was willing to undertake the role of emptying the septic, bucket by miserable bucket. However, before we could do that we had to locate the septic tank. That in itself was quite a task, but find it we did. It was not a pleasant time, but we were able to count it as joy to respond to the calling of the Lord and do anything, including the humblest and most distasteful acts, that God's work might be established. The kinds of sacrifices that were made by all the staff reminded me that the saints, when they are redeemed in God's kingdom, will declare, "Heaven is cheap enough." I do not recall one person discussing the sacrifices that they were making. So focused were all upon the mission that God had called them to fulfill that what may now look like sacrifice was then deemed privilege: working for the Lord and for the mission to which He had called us in beginning the work of Hartland Institute.

# 11 The "Strangers"

*Now when Jesus was born in Bethlehem of Judæa in the days of Herod the king, behold, there came wise men from the east to Jerusalem. . . . And when they were come into the house, they saw the young child with Mary his mother, and fell down, and worshipped him: and when they had opened their treasures, they presented unto him gifts; gold, and frankincense, and myrrh.*
—Matthew 2:1, 11

ELP came from unexpected sources, from those not of our faith. When Hartland Institute was established the Associated Press office in Richmond, Virginia, placed a sizeable story on its wire. This news reached many people. A segment of it was reported in *USA Today*, the national daily newspaper of America. Thus many who would not have known about the inauguration of the institution became acquainted with it. Two men in the Tidewater area of Virginia, about three hours drive from Hartland, were among those who read of the Institute. One Sunday I entered the mansion where one of our staff was escorting a man and his wife around the mansion. I greeted them and the staff member introduced me to them. The man was a physician and his wife a nurse. It was evident that they were not Seventh-day Adventists. As I passed a few words with them, the doctor took out his checkbook saying, "I would like to give you something to help you in this new venture." He then wrote a check for one thousand dollars—a greatly needed thousand dollars in those early days of Hartland Institute.

However, they were soon on their way, and I felt grieved that I had not discovered more about this couple. I learned that he was a physician at the Norfolk Naval Base. From his check I learned his name, Dr. Carl Root. In my mind were questions why he and his wife had decided to make a seven-hour round trip to visit this very new institution which at the time did not even have a college operating? Why, I queried, did he decide to present me with the thousand-dollar check? I believed that I had missed a golden opportunity to learn a little more about him and his interest in Hartland. I took it for granted that as a physician he was especially interested in the health focus of the new institution. But he gave no clue as to the reason he and his wife were there.

Once again God was good. Four weeks later, again on a Sunday afternoon, the same doctor visited us, this time alone. I offered a brief prayer asking the Lord to help me discover more about this man and why he would make a second visit to this very immature institution. This time I asked the right questions, "Doctor, I am intrigued to know why you are interested in this new venture." I was startled by his reply. There was a lengthy pause before he responded, "I am a Loma Linda graduate. For quite a number of years I was a physician at the Reading Rehab (Seventh-day Adventist institution in Pennsylvania) and later at the Brunswick Adventist Hospital in Maine. About fifteen years ago I left the church." By the time this short dialogue had taken place he had already given me yet another one thousand dollar check for the institution.

My mind focused not so much upon the donation, but upon the soul of this man who had once walked in the light, but for fifteen years had followed a path of darkness. With a pleading voice I said to him, "Doctor, thank you so much for your donation and support for Hartland, but far more important to me is your soul's salvation. I believe the Lord has brought you here to help you return to His church." The doctor literally began to shake and eventually in a quavering voice he said, "I know God wants me back in His church."

What a wonderful opportunity to minister to the aching soul of this precious man who was then in his late fifties. I do not know what led him to leave the Seventh-day Adventist church. His wife was not his first wife. She was a member of another denomination. I assured him that my prayers would be for him and that I would pray that he would return to the fellowship of the Lord.

Can you imagine my surprise and delight when, about three months later, I was preaching at the Portsmouth Church in the Tidewater area of Virginia, and observed this physician sitting in the church. Overjoyed, I learned that this was the very day he would be brought back into the fellowship of God's church. This was a gift of infinite price, for I believe that the two thousand dollars was nothing compared with the eternal joy that this man will have in the kingdom of heaven. He continued to support Hartland, though the wife showed no more interest in the project. He soon declared that he would donate his Cadillac to Hartland Institute. However the donation was delayed until the 1979 diesel engine had been replaced by the manufacturer. It became a most valuable part of Hartland's tiny, early fleet. It served us for many years. It was the best vehicle we had and was used to travel to many of our preaching appointments. We always felt, however, compelled to explain to the church members where we preached, the reason we possessed such an expensive car, lest they suspect us of extravagant use of the Lord's funds. In our first year we also received donations of two other vehicles, a utility truck and an old jeep.

Doctor Root became a member of our Institute constituency and was a regular attendee at Hartland's meetings. Sadly, still in his sixties, he contracted Lou Gehrig's disease and succumbed to its degenerative effects. Yet we could not mourn as others, knowing that here was a man who had been reclaimed by the Savior before he passed to his rest. During his connection with Hartland he developed an especially close friendship with Dr. James Drexler, a long time Hartland Board member, whom he knew from Brunswick Adventist Hospital where they had ministered together.

It was not only Doctor Root who had read the newspaper report of the opening of Hartland Institute of Health and Education. One morning, as I was working in my office, I received a phone call from the city of Newport News, also in the Tidewater area of Virginia, the voice that of a very old man. I later was to discover that he was a man seventy-one years old who had been partially debilitated by a stroke. He introduced himself as Lionel Haney, explaining that he had read concerning the opening of Hartland Institute in the Newport News newspaper and that he was very interested in what we were planning to establish. He further stated that he desired to come to visit if we were agreeable. Before I could answer he added, "But I am not a Seventh-day Adventist. However, my mother is." I was amazed to know his mother was still alive. She was a lady in her nineties, a very faithful Seventh-day Adventist. I told Mr. Haney everyone was welcome to visit Hartland and that we would be delighted if he came. He then said, "I have a friend whom I would like to bring with me who also is not a Seventh-day Adventist, but is a Methodist." I said, "By all means, bring your friend." A day for visitation was set.

His friend proved to be Attorney David Murray, a man then in his late forties. I enjoyed their company for three hours as I showed them around the facility. They made favorable comments and showed an interest in what we were doing, but they left, simply saying they had appreciated the tour and they wished us well in our new venture.

However, to our great surprise, a few weeks later I received a letter from Attorney Murray detailing that both he and Mr. Haney were putting up fifty thousand dollars each into an account which would yield eighteen percent per annum. Interest rates were still very high at that time, but even so, eighteen percent was an unusually high yield. He explained that this would continue for two years; every month we would receive a dividend of fifteen hundred dollars. We decided that this money would be put aside for any medical needs and emergencies that might occur with the staff and their families. What a wonderful blessing this was to us, coming totally unexpectedly from men, neither of whom was a part of God's remnant church. We should not have been surprised, for God had said that there would be those not of our faith who would contribute to the work which God has called us to do. Here were two men willing to do so.

> I am greatly encouraged to believe that many persons not of our faith will help considerably by their means.     —*Evangelism*, p. 379

> Sometimes He [God] works through unbelievers, and unexpected relief comes. The Lord puts it into the hearts of men to help.
> —*Welfare Ministry*, p. 279

> The Lord God of Israel has placed His goods in the hands of unbelievers, but they are to be used in favor of doing the works that must be done for a fallen world.     —*Testimonies to Ministers*, p. 203

More than that, Mr. Haney donated quite separately, eighteen thousand dollars, so that we could develop a commercial kitchen in the mansion in a way suitable for the quantity cooking which was much needed for the school. Later still he provided two thousand dollars toward the purchase of a commercial lawn mower. Attorney Murray said he was willing to pay the principal and interest for the purchase of a large tractor. The secondhand tractor was purchased at a cost of seventeen thousand dollars. Attorney Murray paid the loan payments every month until his untimely death. How wonderfully God brought men not of our faith to our aid, as He said He would, to help in the needs which established the work of Hartland.

> There are many not of our faith who will willingly help a work for the uplifting of humanity.     —*General Conference Bulletin*, April 25, 1901

Later Attorney Murray agreed to take the fifty thousand dollars worth of bonds donated to Hartland by Dr. Hart. These bonds would not mature until 1996 and 2006. Dr. Hart had donated these bonds to purchase the one hundred eighty-seven acres on the south of County Road 614 which were part of the original property of Hartland Hall Plantation. In lieu of receiving these bonds Attorney Murray said he would pay the other three thousand dollars per quarter which was necessary to purchase this additional property. Hartland was greatly blessed by these men.

Without any comment, after the two years which Mr. Haney and Attorney Murray had promised to send us $1500 monthly, we continued to receive monthly $750 for a further two years. Then, without notice, the payments stopped. This led us to many queries. I had earlier telephoned Attorney Murray for counsel and advice, but now when I telephoned I was always told that he was not available. I left messages for him to return my calls but he never did return them. I could not explain the turnabout for this man had been kind and very approachable.

We sensed something had changed. Then I received a letter from his sister with the shocking news that Attorney Murray had committed suicide. She briefly elaborated, saying that he had fallen into very serious financial reverses and allegedly some of the efforts which he had made to stop the hemorrhaging were illegal and he was sought by the FBI for fraud. Rather than face the disgrace and the probable lengthy prison term, he ended his life. How we grieved over the death of Attorney Murray, whom God had used to help us in the early days with our financial needs. We wondered how we could have better ministered to this man. Now we knew why suddenly the seven hundred and fifty dollar payments had ceased, as had also the payments on the tractor and on the one hundred and eighty-seven acres of land. However, he had already covered the value of the bonds before his demise, and we were well toward the completion of the payment on the tractor. God found other ways to help us both with our medical fund and the completing of the payments on the additional property and the tractor

The last time we saw Mr. Haney was not long before the death of Attorney Murray. We soon could not trace him and I believe that he probably had died though we received no notice. Through the sadness of this experience, nevertheless, we had seen the handiwork of God helping His new institution along its journey to train young people, to heal the sick, to spread the gospel truth and to proclaim the message of salvation to the world.

I can never forget the families who decorated, carpeted, and furnished two of the Health Center guest rooms. Nor will I forget the donation of furniture for the lobby and for the dining room, (Brother and Sister Ed Martin). Just as valuable was the presentation of a new commercial dishwashing machine (Brother and Sister Garwin McNeilus). There were also denominational institutions (including the Sanitarium Church attached to the Washington Adventist Hospital) which donated office furnishings, pulpit furniture, desks and chairs. It is said that the pulpit furnishings were used at the time Sister White preached in that church.

One of our week of prayer speakers, Elder Leo van Dolson, purchased a much needed portable white board. Others sent books for the college library. Still others either donated or loaned farm and lawn equipment. One of our students combined with Mr. Haney to purchase a fine commercial lawn mower. These are a few illustrations of the gracious help received from so many to assist the development of Hartland. That generosity has never ceased.

We also honor our greatly appreciated volunteer workers. Among the many volunteers, perhaps one stands out—the late Brother Bill Kaiser. Bill spent countless days and weeks using his skills in cutting wood, helping with the grounds, and playing an important role in the beautification of the campus in those early years. The late Roy "Grandpa" Schoonard, the father of Earl, our first plant service director, though in his late eighties, employed his carpentry skills. His energy inspired all the staff. The husband and wife team of the McCormacks was invaluable—"Mac" as a painter, and Lois helped in the business office. How could Hartland have succeeded without the late Bill Perry and his wife, of Pennsylvania? Bill made frequent trips to help with electrical needs. Mr. and Mrs. Don Moon, from Michigan, gave invaluable assistance, first as volunteers and then as staff. He served in building and maintenance, and she as an excellent housekeeper of the mansion before her untimely death from cancer. She was the first staff member to die on Hartland campus.

Some of the greatest blessings have come from neighbors who graciously assisted our work. A special relationship was established with the neighbors who owned the adjacent property on the south side of Hartland, Lee and his brother, the late Randolf Twyman. These men frequently had lunch at Hartland in our early years. They located important features on the property (Lee lived in one of the homes for a number of years) and ploughed garden plots for us. They also donated a home—once used for farm workers—which we had moved from their property to ours. Thank the Lord for such generous neighbors.

We cannot overlook the contribution of the Harts themselves. The Harts contributed the funds for redecorating the "blue room" in the mansion—a room used for the health guests for several years. The Harts also donated the beautiful antique furniture which originally graced the blue room of the mansion as well as two decorative antique clocks, one of early American and the other of early French design. They also presented two beautiful Italian jardinieres. The Harts demonstrated great generosity to the new Institution.

There were many other volunteers—plasterers, teachers, agriculturists, artists and carpenters of general skills. There were still others such as Bill Pruitt, not only a lively member of the Capital Health Center board, but a man who worked tirelessly along with others to redecorate the Capital Health Center, making it ready to serve its clients. He also spent a number of days painting at Hartland.

The half has not been told. God has moved upon many different people in many ways to add to the success of Hartland's beginnings. To all, these sacrificial volunteers and later volunteers, Hartland offers sincere thankfulness and gratitude.

# 12   The Struggles

*And he said, Hearken ye, all Judah, and ye inhabitants of Jerusa-*
*lem, and thou king Jehoshaphat, Thus saith the LORD unto you,*
*Be not afraid nor dismayed by reason of this great multitude; for*
*the battle is not yours, but God's.*               —2 Chronicles 20:15

I can personally testify that for my own spiritual growth I needed to be part of Hartland Institute. It has often been said that the leader of any organization or enterprise bears a much greater burden than any one else in the organization. I had been Academic Dean at West Indies College before becoming president, and immediately I felt the much heavier responsibilities in moving from the number two to the number one role.

At Columbia Union College that situation occurred again, and once again I realized that the leadership role was far beyond the responsibility of the number two role. Yet this was the calling  which I believed God had led me to assume in this new institution. I acknowledge, however, that in the twenty years I have led Hartland, under the great Leader, Jesus Himself, I have had to do much growing. For six years as a young man I taught at the University of Sydney. That required minimal responsibility. When, after completing my studies at the University of Sydney, I accepted the call to join the faculty of Avondale College in 1965, the responsibilities were far greater because now I was working directly in the service of the Lord. The responsibilities were not simply those of teaching or leading an academic department, they now included that of modeling the role of Christ and nurturing the spiritual needs of the more than one hundred and seventy students who were in the Education Department at Avondale College at that time.

These responsibilities continued and increased as further leadership roles were placed upon me. When, in answer to the call of God, I accepted the invitation to join self-supporting work in 1978, the challenges were significantly greater. Now I realized that God was raising up lay ministries with a special focus, in a solemn time of earth's history, to help prepare a people to meet their God. Yes, I had felt that responsibility in denominational work, but it intensified greatly when I joined self-supporting work. Further, there were few controversies to address while teaching at a secular university, and I found that our fellow Seventh-day Adventists highly respected me for the positions I held at the University. When I accepted the call to reenter denominational work, it seemed Satan's challenges were much greater. So much more was at stake in the training of young people, not for professions, careers, occupations or jobs, but for the service of the King of kings and Lord of lords, and those responsibilities weighed heavily upon me.

Yet it was more than this. Somehow in Satan's nefarious activities he made sure that there were many potential conflicts which arose from those of like precious faith. They were the challenges of realizing that my understanding of the call of Christ and of the truth of God was significantly different from that of some of my colleagues, which disparity created serious difficulties. However, even that discord did not compare with the challenges from my beloved brethren and sisters once I had accepted the call to self-supporting work. It seemed that so many who appeared to have affirmed my ministry in denominational work, were now wary, in some cases hostile, to a work they did not understand. I found that many of my fellow ministers, with whom I had shared very cordial fellowship while leading a denominational college, now seemed to view me as a traitor to the cause of God's church. How different was my perception. I believed that the acceptance of responsibility in self-supporting work did nothing to diminish my loyalty to God and His church. In many ways I felt closer to the Lord and the Seventh-day Adventist Church.

Naturally I expected challenges. At first it was difficult to accept the change from being a man highly respected and generally well received by his brethren and sisters, to having to face stern criticism, unkind comments, false rumors and malicious gossip. However, this was exactly what I needed to help in the refinement of my character. Christ warned,

Woe unto you, when all men shall speak well of you!    —Luke 6:26

When, generally speaking, we are praised and honored, it is unlikely that our spiritual growth can mature. When there are no tests, when there are no trials, we do not know how fully we have dedicated our lives to the Lord. I had to learn, through sometimes bitter experiences, that we must do all to the glory of God and not for the praise of men. I had to learn never to be hurt, never to be bitter, never to be negative nor reactive to what others thought of me. These lessons are not easy to learn, and there is still much room for growth, but I believe that, step by step, the Lord is leading me to understand that if we are seeking only the glory of the One who gave His all for us, then we need not be burdened when others seek to question our motives and reputation. After all the Scripture reveals that Jesus is our Example (1 Peter 2:21), and since He—

> made himself [Christ] of no reputation . . .                    —Philippians 2:7

we must follow His lead.

There were other struggles which I discovered. The Scripture says,

> . . . this is the victory that overcometh the world, even our faith.
>                                                           —1 John 5:4

The Scripture further warns,

> But without faith it is impossible to please him: for he that cometh to God must believe that he is, and that he is a rewarder of them that diligently seek him.                        —Hebrews 11:6

> . . . whatsoever is not of faith is sin.                    —Romans 14:23

I needed Hartland, first to demonstrate how weak my faith was, and second to help me to seek daily to receive the faith of Jesus. Much of this struggle was seen in the repeated financial crises which we faced for quite a few years. Each time we faced a financial hurdle my faith wavered. As I reflect on this experience I am reminded of the children of Israel. When they confronted the Red Sea ahead and the army of Pharaoh behind, their angry outburst against Moses showed their faithlessness and their lack of belief that God, who was bringing them out of Egypt, was testing them. Utterly they failed the test. Only Moses stood with unwavering faith. He pled,

> Fear ye not, stand still, and see the salvation of the Lord.
>                                                           —Exodus 14:13

At last when they crossed the Red Sea the ladies, led by Miriam, danced in joy for the deliverance. However it was but a short few days before they were at Marah, where they found the water to be bitter. They had not learned to trust in the Lord. Through many other experiences—when they cried out for food, and again at the rock, they showed their anger and displeasure with human leaders.

God brought them back to the same test. Repeatedly, so weak was their faith, they faltered. Eventually it dawned upon me that I was no better than the Israelites. God had wonderfully and providentially led us to the commencement of Hartland, and yet each time a financial crisis loomed my faith wavered. The Lord had to bring me repeatedly over the same ground. I have learned, I hope well, that when God is testing my faith and I fail the test, I am going to face the same situation again. If I fail that test He will not give up on me, but will confront me with yet another similar test, and so it will continue until I am willing to rest my faith fully and confidently in the Lord.

The first major test came October 1, 1983, when we were facing our first quarterly mortgage payment of just over eighteen thousand dollars. Four days before the payment was to be made, with all our best efforts, we still had little more than seven thousand dollars toward the eighteen thousand. I felt very nervous. "How would we ever make the payment on the appointed day?" But there is a God in heaven. The staff learned to pray earnestly and I joined them. Yet my prayer was not in full faith that God would not fail His work. That same day a retired Swedish psychiatrist, Dr. Anders, called to indicate that he had heard that we had a payment to make shortly and he was sending five hundred dollars to help. He told me that he would contact another Swedish physician, a man known very well to many faithful Seventh-day Adventists, Dr. Lloyd Rosenvold. Dr. Rosenvold called and said he would also contribute five hundred dollars. That meant we still needed ten thousand dollars. However, Dr. Rosenvold said there was a farmer, Jerry Eller, in Montana who might be willing to help and he would contact him to explain our need.

A couple of hours later I received a call from the farmer who declared that a wonderful thing had happened. The day before, he had received a tax rebate of about five thousand dollars from the Internal Revenue Service. That very morning he and his wife had decided to dedicate that rebate to the work of God and they prayed that God would guide them as to where to send the money. They scarcely were off their knees when Dr. Rosenvold called and they believed that their prayer was answered. They promised to wire the five thousand dollars the same day. I now knew that God was answering our prayers mightily in spite of my feeble faith.

By the time the money was needed we had received a check from a physician in California for four thousand five hundred dollars and two ladies, one in Maryland and one in Tennessee had each sent checks of one thousand dollars. Praising God, we were able to pay our first mortgage payment in full and on time.

The Lord knew, however, that I had failed the faith test. Three months later the test was repeated. On New Year's day 1984, one day before the second mortgage payment was due, I had been informed that we had about eight thousand dollars in reserves for the payment. It just seemed to me impossible that we could find ten thousand dollars by the next day. Brother Mayer and I had been in California for the first Hartland Bible Conference, which concluded on Sunday morning. After returning to Washington, D.C., I called Dr. Dennis Blum, Dean of the College, from a phone booth and he gave us the solemn news. I felt a fear that evidenced itself in a squeamish feeling in the abdomen. It seemed impossible that we could find the ten thousand dollars. But as I walked out of the public phone booth the Holy Spirit mightily convicted me of my faithlessness. Then and there I confessed my faithlessness and told the Lord I was convinced that He would have the additional ten thousand dollars by the next day. A check for ten thousand dollars arrived the next day from a farmer in Oklahoma, Alvin Meier, and once again we were able to meet the mortgage payment on time. Brother Meier had sent the check from Oklahoma before that prayer had been uttered. God had answered the prayer before it was made. God had mercifully answered, even in spite of my weak but growing faith.

Miracle after miracle happened, but my faith still continued to fail me. In 1988, when we had returned from an overseas trip which will be addressed later in this book, I was met with a large number of very worried and hostile staff members saying that we were well over two hundred thousand dollars in operational debt. Once again, my heart failed. Even when I discovered that the debt was actually one hundred and forty-six thousand dollars, I knew at this early stage in the development of Hartland, that could be a crippling debt and could lead to the collapse of the Institution. I knew that statistics confirmed that in the United States more than half of start-up enterprises close within their first five years of operation. It could lead to the bankruptcy of the institution five years after its beginning. Why did my faith fail? God had never let us down before, and once again our patient Savior came through. One man wrote a check for the entire debt, saying he desired to give us a new financial start. If any of our readers doubt that there is a God in heaven or believe that miracles are confined to biblical times, you have not known of the experience of Hartland Institute.

Yet I would estimate it took me about another five years before I fully determined that, come what may, I would never again question or doubt the providence of God when we were facing difficulties of any kind. It was then, and only then, that God removed from me and from the institution these recurring, desperate financial situations. Yes, there is a God in heaven. He loves us so much that He will test and try us until we surmount our character weaknesses. No wonder Peter could say,

[He is] not willing that any should perish, but that all should come to
repentance.                                                              —2 Peter 3:9

A word for the reader—If you find yourself facing repeatedly the
same test and trial, it is almost certain evidence that you have failed the
test, and in His love and mercy God is providing further opportunities for
you to surmount the test through faith in Him. The only other possibility is
that, we having passed an easier test, He is testing us with a much
stronger one.

# 13 The College

*And they were astonished at his doctrine: for he taught them as one that had authority, and not as the scribes.* —Mark 1:22

FIRST and foremost the goal of Hartland Institute is to educate young men and women from around the world to be leaders to contribute to the completion of the gospel commission. We look for young people, in this age where greed, selfishness, materialism, entertainment and careers dominate young minds, who will surrender all for Jesus Christ and work for Him. The servant of the Lord gave us our marching orders.

> With such an army of workers as our youth, rightly trained, might furnish, how soon the message of a crucified, risen, and soon-coming Saviour might be carried to the whole world! —*Education*, p. 271

Ellen White has given us much hope that there will be such young people, for she declared that it will be largely the youth who will finish the work of God.

> In the closing scenes of this earth's history many of these children and youth will astonish people by their witness to the truth, which will be borne in simplicity, yet with spirit and power. . . . In the near future many children will be endued with the Spirit of God and will do a work in proclaiming the truth to the world that at that time cannot well be done by the older members of the church. —*Adventist Home*, p. 489

Our human instinct was to wonder who would come to this new, untried school? From where would they come? How many would there be? We soon discovered that inquiries do not necessarily translate into enrolled students. In the end there were fourteen students who enrolled during the first year—seven men and seven women. Five were from Virginia, three from California, two from Ohio, two from Georgia and one each from Oklahoma and Florida. These were to comprise the pioneer student body. Of course, they had to experience many sacrifices, too. But in many ways they received an education that the present students, who are no longer privileged to pioneer, cannot duplicate. With such a small body of students they were very important and their education very personal.

These first students formed a privileged group. They had come to our college, which had yet to establish its fine reputation as an institution in which young people may train in excellence, receiving the finest valid Christian education in the world field. But God rewarded their faith for they were the privileged few. They received a blessing which God bestowed.

It was not possible for us to enroll foreign students requiring student visas because, like all beginning institutions, we had no status with the Immigration Department that we might do so. We immediately worked diligently upon this issue. Dr. Dennis Blum, first Dean of the College, and I worked together to see if we could achieve the status necessary to bring foreign students to the college. It was our goal to enroll young people from around the world who were willing to be trained so that they could return to their homelands to commence similar ministries. Obtaining the appropriate immigration status was not a simple matter. I had been responsible for some necessary legwork in obtaining this status for Weimar College, and it had proven quite difficult. One of the strict regulations was that until student credits have been accepted by three accredited colleges or universities, no application for authorization to accept foreign students would be considered. Quite obviously this placed a new institution in a dilemma. The staff did not desire to lose students to another institution. Yet, on the other hand, that must happen before application can be made. Eventually we had been successful at Weimar, but not until we had surmounted many difficulties. It was evident that the Lord had blessed us.

At Hartland College we had to begin all over again. One advantage I had was my Weimar experience. Dr. Blum and I visited the Federal Department of Education in Washington. We were surprised and very disappointed at the curt and uncooperative response of the officer who said there was no way that they would be interested in reviewing an application from an institution so new and so small. By this time we did have three students who had transferred to three different institutions. I explained to the officer what had happened at Weimar and how we had received acceptance of our application. He was unmoved by that precedent. He told us that it was very rare that an unaccredited educational institution would receive such certification.

This left us again with only one further avenue we could pursue—the Immigration and Naturalization Service.

We dealt with a very cooperative man at the Immigration office attached to the Washington-Dulles International Airport. Very frankly we explained what had happened at the Department of Education, and I also related my experience with the INS in Sacramento which, in spite of the fact that the Education Department of the Federal Government had refused to consider our application, INS had certified Weimar to receive overseas students. This explanation seemed to produce the desired effect. While he was still somewhat hesitant, he opened the door. "I will visit your institution and make my decision on that inspection." Once again the mighty arm of prayer was moving to help us. By the grace of God he came, visited, interviewed and expressed his satisfaction with the facilities, and promised to do what he could. We believe he wanted to be sure that we were not a fly-by-night school which would fail to provide a legitimate academic environment. Soon thereafter we received verbal and then written certification to receive overseas students commencing with the winter quarter of 1985, when our first students with student visas, Victor Gilbert and Sophie Govarin, arrived from Bermuda and Australia respectively, and God had opened the heart of an immigration officer to do His will on behalf of His work. As of the twentieth school year we have had students from forty-eight foreign countries. Many of them are back in their homeland areas working for God. Some have established ministries which are reaching many souls.

In 2003 the Lord greatly blessed our dedication to follow the voice of God and His voice alone. After 9/11 officers chosen by the Immigration and Naturalization Service inspected all colleges and universities in the United States who accepted foreign students. Hartland College received an excellent report and passed every category. However, because the College was not accredited, we were required to have evidence that our student academic credits had been accepted unconditionally by at least three accredited institutions when students tranferred. The Hartland College Dean, Joong Ho Shin, along with the College Director of Admissions, Thomas Heath, and I prayed together promising God that, no matter what the outcome, we would not dishonor Him by seeking human accreditation.

After a telephone dialog with an INS officer we received our recertification without submitting letters from any colleges or universities affirming that our students' credits had been accepted. Once again, God confirmed His divine guidance in Hartland Institute.

At the end of the first school year we held our first graduation. The first graduate was Regina Young from Florida. She had been a student at Laurelbrook and Weimar (two years) and decided to complete her final year, majoring in Christian Elementary Education, at the new institution. Small though the graduation class, consisting of only one student, a very blessed experience it proved to be. Regina had undertaken most of her college work prior to attending Hartland. She had not only completed her classroom studies, but had distinguished herself in work education, out-reach ministries, and had excelled in her student teaching at the Ontario Seventh-day Adventist School in California.

The college had planned a simple but impressive Wednesday evening service. Members of Regina's family were present from Florida. The local Seventh-day Adventist churches supported the graduation by the attendance of many of their members, as well as a number of neighbors and friends. The graduation was highlighted by the testimony as presented by Regina and several other students. Dr. Blum outlined the purposes of Christian education, and I challenged Regina and those present with the life of Ruth as a worthy example to all young women.

In each of the next two years there was one graduate. Pam Hamman, the 1985 graduate, was the wife of the Food Service Director, who also had completed a considerable amount of her studies at Weimar College. She graduated with a major in Health Ministries. In 1986 our third graduate was Stephen DeLong. He graduated from the Pastoral Evangelism major and is now an ordained minister and for many years was an evangelist with Amazing Facts.

Our graduation which included the first four-year graduates took place in 1987. The graduates were Brent Amos, Timothy Bailey, Dawn Blum, Guillermo Bonilla, Jill Hines, Elizabeth Holland-Wright, Timothy Jo, Barry Katzer, Laura Mayer, Paula Morris, Kimbra Rockwell, Marcia Rockwell, Nila Teale, and Wayne Wright. The first three graduations were simple single night ceremonies, held in the college chapel. The fourth graduation was held out of doors by the large pillars of the mansion, with family, guests, staff and students seated on chairs facing the mansion. As has been the practice ever since, there was no major ceremony for the distribution of diplomas. At the very first graduation, the emphasis was not upon the achievements and accomplishments of the graduates, but rather upon the wonderful mercies and blessings of God which have brought the graduates to this stage of their preparation for God's work. Further emphasis is placed upon the calling of God upon the lives and service of the graduates. This principle has been followed at every subsequent graduation. Thus the diplomas were handed out at a private service involving a few family members and occasionally a few friends, prior to the commencement of the graduation ceremony. This practice follows the graduations at Healdsburg College (the predecessor of Pacific Union College) which was positively endorsed by Sister White (*Fundamentals of Christian Education*, p. 487). Graduates of Hartland College honor their alma mater, *not* by donating large contributions to the alumni funds, but by wholehearted surrender of their all to Jesus Christ and to the service of mankind, readying themselves to be part of the final generation who will be prepared to receive the latter rain, to proclaim the gospel under Pentecostal power to the world and to lead many souls to the kingdom of eternity.

I cannot conclude this chapter without acknowledging the initial teaching staff. Pastor David Grams, Bible; Dr. John Goley, Health; Mrs. Betsy Mayer, English; Dr. Carl Anderson, History; Mr. Ken Flemmer, Vegetable Gardening; Dr. Dennis Blum, Marriage and the Family; Elder Milo Sawvel, Outreach. I taught Philosophy of Christian Education. Acknowledgment is also due to the subsequent College Deans, Dr. Keith Anderson; and after I had carried the role for three years assisted by Betsy Mayer, Hal Mayer and the present dean, Joong Ho Shin.

Hartland College exists to serve God and man. The privilege to train students is the central focus of the mission of Hartland Institute.

One of the most enduring results of Hartland's first year was the reestablishing of the student colporteur summer program. This did not begin from a staff initiative but with the dedication of a freshman student, Timothy Bailey from Ohio. Tim had been an enthusiastic colporteur while a student at Mount Vernon Academy in a program led by Larry Carter.

Very early into the initial school year Tim was urging administration to begin a colporteur outreach. Finally I told him that if such a program was to begin he should lead it. Tim took no second urging. The program began Sunday afternoon and by the close of the first year he had arranged for Larry to lead a most successful summer program. This gave great encouragement to the leaders of the literature work at the Review and Herald Publishing Association, especially Brother Dick Thomas.

The following year a number of our students were asked to visit some of our denominational institutions and thus began the revitalization of the summer colporteur program. Subsequently, winter programs also have been initiated by Hartland College with considerable success. Indirectly the more recent establishments of colporteur training schools can be traced to this resurrection of the colporteur summer program. Timothy Bailey, now an ordained minister, is presently teaching and leading the colporteur ministry at Union Springs Academy in upstate New York.

# 14    The Health Program

*Beloved, I wish above all things that thou mayest prosper and be in health, even as thy soul prospereth.*        —3 John 2

IT took longer than expected to commence the ministry of the Hartland Health Center (now known as Hartland Wellness Center). The staff was in place. Dr. Warren Peters, the Director, was joined by Drs. Gayle Wilson and Everett Kuester. The center also had two trained nurses, Linda Ball and Ronda Potterton; a trained dietician, Heather Houck; and a trained health educator, Dr. John Goley. The Dean of the College, Dr. Dennis Blum, also had a doctorate in Health Science; Hal Mayer was a trained respiratory therapist and health educator, and his wife, Betsy, was a trained nurse. These all were ready to help out if needed. We had an outstanding team.

The delay, however, was caused by the need to prepare a portion of the mansion to serve as the initial Health Center unit. A section of the second floor of the mansion, where four commodious rooms were located, was chosen as the initial accommodation area for the Hartland Health Center. Serious repairs had to be completed to the rooms because of water damage caused by broken pipes, and each room had to be well painted and fitted out with appropriate furniture. Each room and the hallway had to be recarpeted. Each room had its distinctive characteristics—respectively the rooms were painted pink, blue, green and rust. A small hydrotherapy room and doctor's office were fitted out at the far end of the second floor. A family from New Market, Virginia, Brother and Sister Morton, lovingly volunteered to take the responsibility to renovate and paint while also paying for the cost of supplies for redecorating the pink room. Dr. John Hart, one of the former owners, paid for the cost of renovating the blue room and provided antique furniture for it. From other donations we completed the renovations.

Long before the opening of Hartland Institute, the search for a medical director had focused upon Dr. Warren Peters. Dr. and Mrs. Peters readily made the commitment to Hartland, and long before their official call arrived, Dr. Peters had been laying a firm foundation for the new health program. Soon after the arrival of the medical team in August 1983, the health program was slated to begin. As already described, this date proved unrealistic because of the major renovations and the remodeling necessary for the commencement of the program. It was May of 1984 before the first live-in patients could be accepted. Dr. Warren Peters was succeeded as director of the Wellness Center by Rick Mautz, Jeff Barbieri, Will Evert, Dr. Yew-Por Ng and the present director, Walt Cross.

While forging the live-in program, Dr. Peters was also negotiating with the Hyattsville, Maryland, Seventh-day Adventist Church for the operation of an outpatient clinic, to be named the Capital Health Center. The Capital Health Center was located in the commodious facilities adjacent to the Hyattsville church. The two-storey building had been built in the 1930s at the inspiration of Elder F. D. Nichol, long time editor of the *Review and Herald*. Used for many years as a clinic for less-advantaged people, it was staffed by Washington Adventist Hospital and Leland Memorial Hospital. Closed for a number of years, it had been later used for Pathfinder Clubs and other church activities.

Some time before the commencement of Hartland Institute, Dr. Marshall Grosboll, holding a doctorate in Health Science, became the pastor of that church and planned to begin a strong health ministry. He was supported by some church members. The upper story of the clinic had been renovated with a fine lecture room and kitchen equipment for cooking schools and other activities. The downstairs, however, required major remodeling.

After careful negotiations between Hartland, Hyattsville Seventh-day Adventist Church and the Potomac Conference of Seventh-day Adventists, an agreement was signed to use the facility as an outpatient clinic. The renovation of the lower floor of the building was a joint venture between Hartland and the Hyattsville Church with the help of several generous donations from Hartland friends, including ten thousand dollars from a donor in the Northwest. Designed as a city clinic to assist city dwellers, it was also to be used as a base for referrals to the live-in program of the Hartland Health Center. In this way it fulfilled the counsel of the Lord which calls for city treatment rooms associated with a sanitarium located in a rural area.

While the medical team planned and assisted in the development of the facilities for the Hartland Health Center, they were active in medical missionary work. The medical team engaged in health seminars, cooking schools and stop-smoking clinics. These were conducted in Hyattsville, Maryland; Culpeper and Charlottesville, Virginia; Reading, Pennsylvania; and also in Idaho. The team also assisted with health lectures at Orange and Fredericksburg, Virginia. Further, they participated in health fairs held in the Washington, D.C. area.

The official opening of the Capital Health Center took place Sunday and Monday, February 13–14, 1984. For five years the clinic offered quality lifestyle medical care. Later a second clinic was opened, attached to the Charlottesville Seventh-day Adventist School. Dr. Gayle Wilson was assisted by dietician Heather Houck in this clinic.

It was on May 6, 1984, that Hartland Health Center went into high gear with the opening of its live-in program. Staff and students worked tirelessly to meet the spring deadline. The pressure fell heavily upon Linda Ball, who was responsible for coordinating the preparations. Betsy Mayer and Heather Houck were in the dietary department. Dr. John Goley was not only head of the Health Ministries Department of the College, but head of the plumbing, too. Dennis Blum, College Dean, coordinated the final thrust to finish the painting of rooms and the follow-up after Darlis Schoonard fell ill. Earl Schoonard and his construction workers quickly accomplished a multitude of tasks, from installing hot water to making sure the electrical needs were met. Business Manager Rich Moseanko, in conjunction with Earl Schoonard and physician Everett Kuester, worked diligently to isolate and repair water pipes to ensure a good water supply to the mansion. Others busily dug the trenches for the sewage drain field. I was part of the latter team: it was an all-out effort.

Indeed, the accomplishments in the two weeks prior to the opening of the health program were well-nigh miraculous. All worked with a tremendous purpose, culminating in a final push the day the health guests arrived. A special donation of forty thousand dollars by Mr. O. D. McKee made the goal achievable, for this money provided means to drill an additional water well and provided finances to finish the Health Center area of the mansion. The first well was drilled beyond four hundred feet without producing water. The second site produced a steady flow of about five gallons per minute at about eighty feet.

Not everything was in place for our first two live-in guests, one from Orlando, Florida and the other from Georgia. There were problems with water supply in the first few days, but the loving, expert care of the health team made up for the inconveniences. The patients' understanding inspired the staff, and the significant improvement in the health of the guests made all the effort worthwhile.

Before the end of the first year at Hartland, a second health program had commenced. What a great delight to the Hartland family to have Dr. and Mrs. John Hart among the four guests. With them were Dr. Hart's sister, Grace McMahn, and a retired space engineer from Ohio, Bill Alexander. The excellent response of all four to the health program was thrilling. Bill, a bypass surgery patient, was walking briskly eleven miles each day toward the end of the program. Dr. Hart's cardiac problems also showed marked improvement.

It was a joy to hear the Harts tell stories of the history and development of the property. Pearl Hart even assisted in showing visitors the mansion. She graciously explained some of the details that were unfamiliar to the staff. As the guests were leaving from a side door she said, "Don't forget to come again." She was for a moment reliving her past experiences.

The health program is designed to relieve disease and improve the health of patients suffering from atherosclerosis, hypertension, arthritis, diabetes, obesity, cancer and other lifestyle diseases. It is established upon the eight simple treatment modalities ordained by God.

In the middle ages, sudden death, as occurs in heart attack, was known as "noblemen's disease." The reason was simple: the serfs lived a plain healthful life with ample exercise in the open air, and a simple, mainly vegetarian diet. The lords of the manor ate rich foods and took little exercise outside of sports as youth. They largely confined themselves to indoor activities and a "luxurious" diet. While the serfs died of infectious diseases, the lords frequently died from heart attacks and strokes.

Today many, even of the lower economic segment of society, live the lifestyle of the nobility of the middle ages. Thus, heart disease and strokes are endemic. Wherever Western lifestyle has been accepted, death from these causes has increased dramatically. The health program at Hartland is designed to teach guests the simple way to improve the quality of their lives. With many confined to predominantly sedentary occupations in the city and suburban areas, while eating food which is predominantly refined and free of much-needed fiber and far too rich in saturated fats, there is no mystery why lifestyle diseases are common today.

At Hartland Health Center, physicians constantly monitor the progress of guests, and as their physical condition improves, they reduce the amount of medication given. Some advance so fast that they are free of all medication by the end of the eighteen-day program. Others have greatly reduced their medications during the same time period.

The natural remedies used by the medical staff conveniently fit an acronym made from the name HARTLAND:

**H** *ydrotherapy*
**A** *ir*
**R** *est*
**T** *emperance*
**L** *ight*
**A** *ctivity*
**N** *utrition*
**D** *ivine Power*

Each of these treatment modalities is combined with the loving care of a dedicated Christian staff.

Obviously, because of the limited accommodation, it was difficult for us to increase the number of health guests. When at one health session we hosted seven health guests we had virtually reached capacity. The present Wellness Center permits many more health guests to take advantage of this health-improving and restoring program.

# 15   The Wellness Center

*A merry heart doeth good like a medicine: but a broken spirit drieth the bones.*      —Proverbs 17:22

IN the early days of Hartland we had developed a campus master plan. Upon this master plan we had determined the site of the future health center building. We were greatly blessed by the services of Dr. Ray Davidson from Andrews University, who looked kindly upon the ministry of Hartland. He was a qualified surveyor and campus planner. He had helped the campus planning of a number of self-supporting institutions as well as denominational institutions. Dr. Davidson volunteered to spend a couple of weeks and set out the sites of our proposed future buildings. The development of the new building for what is now the Hartland Wellness Center was hindered by the fact that every three months we had to raise more than $18,100 as the quarterly payment against the mortgage. This need made it particularly difficult to raise additional funds for other projects including the new Wellness Center. However, the impetus to become serious about building the Wellness Center came when Brother and Sister O. D. McKee donated first $100,000 and then $200,000 to commence the building.

We had originally planned a wellness center of about sixteen thousand square feet. It was our desire to construct a building with such a design that it would be in harmony with the architecture of the mansion. Thus we planned a brick building with pillars, albeit far less grand than the huge sandstone pillars of the mansion. We dreamed of decorating it graciously and furnishing it tastefully. The decision was made to construct the bottom floor within which would be located the major administrative offices, a lecture room, doctor's office, the nurses' station, male and female therapy rooms, an exercise room, an exercise pool, shower facilities and locker rooms.

On the upper floor the architectural plan called for fifteen commodious motel-style rooms, a number of which would be furnished with queen-size beds and others to be furnished with two double beds. Each room was designed to have its own individual bathroom. Within the plan for the upper floor a small apartment to provide accommodation for a senior staff member was apportioned. Finally, this level was designed to have a multipurpose room where meals could be taken, lectures presented, cooking demonstrations undertaken and evening worship and fellowships could also be conducted. Also on the second floor we incorporated a mezzanine area for other casual activities. The completed area of the building extended to twenty-one thousand square feet.

The preparation of the building site went smoothly. Because of the prevalence of rocks in various parts of the campus we were afraid that we might discover large subterranean rocks as we dug away soil in the area where the building was to be located. By God's grace none was found. The many truckloads of subsoil which were carried away helped to develop the western parking lot, which required huge amounts of fill. The ground having been prepared, we had arrived at the time to lay the concrete slab for the building and to pour concrete for a retaining wall at the northern end of the slab.

As we neared the time for the concrete to be poured, it became imperative that plumbing be installed under the slab. Only two days before we were to subcontract the plumbing job to a local plumber, we received a call from Lynwood and Peggy Spangler. They told us that they were plumbers and just then were between jobs and asked if we could use them as volunteers for a few days! Could we use them? Just in time, they arrived and laid all the plumbing for the building so the slab could be poured. Other blessings mounted. The concrete was donated by Garwin McNeilus, then the largest manufacturer of concrete trucks in the world. Three more years passed by before the Wellness Center was completed.

Later Lynwood Spangler enrolled as a pastoral evangelism major at Hartland. Peggy, for a number of years while he was studying, became a very effective office manager at the Hartland Wellness Center. Today Elder Spangler is an evangelist who, under the power of the Holy Spirit, has led many precious souls to the gospel of Jesus Christ.

We were very thankful when Maranatha Flights International agreed to help us in 1987 with framing and wiring of the building. What a wonderful dedicated group of energetic workers they were. However, to our disappointment and theirs, they were greatly hampered by days of heavy rain while they were undertaking this work, and probably achieved no more that half their goal in spite of the fact they added an extra day to make up some of the lost time caused by the rain. While they were at Hartland, however, they were able to frame the first and second floors.

The cost of constructing the Wellness Center was by no means limited to the building itself. The Madison County Building Inspector and Board of Supervisors, as well as the Virginia State Authority had mandated that we construct a large water storage tower for the distribution of the water to the campus and to help maintain water pressure throughout the whole property. We were also required to provide three-phase power units, and to construct a sewage treatment system. The Wellness Center could not be approved for operation until all these requirements had been met. The requirements added much unbudgeted cost to the building of the Wellness Center. We were very grateful for the assistance provided by Brother Bob Logan. He, with his wife, traveled from Oregon to operate the heavy equipment necessary for the development of the two sewage ponds. Brother Logan also assisted with other heavy equipment work around the campus. When we consider all the volunteers who have helped Hartland over the years, we delight to praise God for these friends who were so willing to sacrifice their time and labor that they might forward God's work at Hartland.

It was not until 1990 that the Wellness Center was completed. On this occasion we held a special grand opening and a service of thanksgiving to God. This opening was held more than three years after the ground-breaking ceremony. Again we had community, state and national leaders or their representatives present at the opening, all of whom expressed their approval of what had been accomplished. These government dignitaries were led by Representative Frank Slaughter, the then member of the House of Representatives for the district in which Hartland Institute is located. All in all, including the other related projects mentioned above, the project cost $1.3 million. That was a huge sum for the fledgling institute. How thankful we are for the donations which helped develop the Hartland Wellness Center, and have facilitated the improved health of so many health guests.

A special tribute has been made to the late Brother and Sister O. D. McKee. Both O. D. and his wife, Ruth, loved Hartland and showed their love in very practical ways. They were later to donate a further half-million dollars toward the project. This was a remarkable answer to desperate prayers. Just prior to the departure of Dr. Peters, Hal Mayer and I to preach in the Far East, the funds for the building were depleted. This led to the decision to stop building. How earnestly we prayed during our itinerating in the Far East. While ministering at Port Dickson, Malaysia, Dr. Peters received the wonderful word of the additional $500,000 donation of the McKees. Also with us on the itinerary were Richard and Laurena Mayer. It would be hard for the reader to imagine the prayers of gratefulness which were raised to the Lord in that far away land. What a wonderful God we serve.

Now unto him that is able to do exceeding abundantly above all that we
ask or think, according to the power that worketh in us. —Ephesians 3:20

But before the Wellness Center could be completed we still required
a further $300,000. To our assistance came Bethel Sanitarium located in
southern Indiana, led by its administrator, David Kast. Bethel Sanitarium
offered to loan the $300,000 needed to complete the project at a low, six
percent interest rate. The board was enthusiastic about accepting this
generous offer. The only vote against it was mine. I was concerned about
such a big debt and the pressure upon our operating funds as we made
those repayments. As I look back I can now confirm that the other board
members were correct and I was wrong.

God blessed mightily, and as we came closer to the completion of
paying off the debt, with wonderful love and consideration for the work of
Hartland, Bethel Sanitarium board voted that, if we could finish the payments by a set date they would forgive all the interest over that previous
year. What a powerful incentive! The challenge was successfully achieved
under the leadership of Ron Goss, the Hartland Institute Development
Director. In addition Bethel Sanitarium actually forgave us the last almost
thirty thousand dollars of the debt. More recently Brother Kast has served
a number of years as a valuable member of the Board of Directors of
Hartland Institute.

How God has used many friends who love the Lord to help establish
the facilities of Hartland. The Wellness Center has been a blessing for
many hundreds of health guests, most of whom may not be well-known
members of the community but who are precious souls for the Lord.
Others have included company directors, some have held high administrative roles in major national or international corporations. Scores of Seventh-day Adventist pastors and some pastors of other denominations have
passed through the Wellness Center. Men who hold church responsibility
on the local Conference level, Union Conference level and the North
American Division level have also been blessed by the restoration that
comes through the use of God's natural remedies. Lawyers and judges,
F.B.I. and State Department employees have passed through the
Wellness Center as well as the Director of Minority Affairs in the (elder)
Bush Administration. One cabinet minister of the national government of
Jamaica was greatly blessed spiritually and physically by the program.
People have come from every inhabited continent to have their health
restored at the Hartland Wellness Center. Our vision, however high,
never can match the reality that God gives when we follow His counsel
and His leading.

# 16 The Publications

*Publications must be multiplied, and scattered like the leaves of autumn. These silent messengers are enlightening and molding the minds of thousands in every country and in every clime.*
—*Review and Herald*, November 21, 1878

HARTLAND Publications had its roots far away from rural Virginia. It commenced in northern California in the city of Paradise in 1977. A group of fourteen brethren and sisters concerned with the erosion of the precious truths that God has entrusted to the Seventh-day Adventist church came in contact with the first publication written to expose the dangers of the "new theology." This book, titled *Conflicting Concepts of Righteousness by Faith in the Seventh-day Adventist Church*, was written by Dr. John Clifford and my brother, Dr. Russell Standish. Considering that they had little more than six weeks to prepare this book, it was a marvelous presentation defending God's truths and exposing the errors that were flooding into the Seventh-day Adventist church in a desperate effort by Satan to destroy its mission and destiny. The book focused upon the errors promoted by Dr. Desmond Ford, the Chairman of the Theology Department of Avondale College, Australia.

The motivation for writing the book, and its timing, were dictated by a General Conference decision to meet with leaders from the South Pacific Division to discuss the specific influence of Desmond Ford and his teachings within the Seventh-day Adventist Church. The meeting was held at Palmdale, California, in 1976. The book was hastened to the General Conference leaders. Both Elder Robert Pierson, General Conference President, and the editor of the *Review and Herald* magazine (now the *Adventist Review*), Elder Kenneth Wood, expressed great appreciation and support for the material contained in that publication. It is interesting that it took two physicians, faithful watchmen on the walls of Zion, to be the first to present in written form the deadly error of the new theology.

The Paradise group sought and gained permission to reprint the book in America. They set up a small organization with headquarters at the home of Dr. Wendell and Lillian Gibbs. Dr. Gibbs was a local dentist who was supported by others including Lowell and Mili Scarbrough, Vern and

Dorothy Kauffman, Bob and Evelyn Green, Dorothy Hilmer, Gordon and Patsy Jester, Vernon and Sally Lavoie, and Dorothy Scarbrough. They stocked books in the garage of Dr. Gibbs' home and called their effort "Historic Truth Publications."

In 1980 Russell and I had finished the manuscript of our first book, *Adventism Vindicated*, but had no funds with which to print it. At a meeting of about sixty people, on the property of Lowell and Mili Scarbrough, financial pledges were made to print the book. By God's grace they raised over five thousand dollars—adequate to print five thousand books. From there they continued to print all the new books which Russell and I wrote including, *Adventism Unveiled* (now titled *Sacrificial Priest*), *Adventism Proclaimed, Adventism Jeopardized* (now titled *God's Solution for Depression, Guilt and Mental Illness*), *Adventism Imperiled* and the two volumes of *Adventism Challenged—The Gathering Storm* and *The Storm Bursts* (now printed in one volume). Historic Truth Publications also published books and papers by such faithful authors as Dr. Ralph Larson, Elder Ron Spear, Dr. Erwin Gane and one of their own members, Brother Lowell Scarbrough.

During the early part of 1984 I received a letter from Dr. Gibbs containing an offer from Historic Truth Publications generously setting forth the willingness of the members of that group to transfer the operation to Hartland Institute. He explained that some of those who had been helping for quite a number of years had moved away from the area. Others were slowing down with increasing age and it seemed appropriate that some more effective organization should be established. He believed that Hartland was the logical home for this publishing house. Some of the Administrative Committee members were reluctant to take on a third division of Hartland at such an early stage of its existence, but in the end it was voted, and ratified by the board of directors, to incorporate this important part of God's work into the ministry of Hartland. Historic Truth Publications sent all its stock of books and a little in excess of eighteen thousand dollars which they held in profits from the sales over the years so that we had start-up funds in order to print more books.

At first the new publishing venture was named Hartland Truth Publications (HTP), but it was quickly simplified to Hartland Publications (HP). It was initially very much a part-time activity. Elder Milo Sawvel, the Director of Development and his assistant, Duane Schoonard, cared for the inventory and the orders. Soon, however, because of a growth in activity, it was seen by administration that Hartland Publications required a permanent staff. Initially the activities were carried on in a small room in the mansion, which was then Elder Sawvel's office. That room is now the education room. When the mechanics' shop was built, a small section was put aside for this growing publishing venture. Hartland Publications eventually grew to the point where it took over most of the mechanics' shop. The mechanics' shop was relocated. For a time Brother Hal Mayer led the operations and then permanent full-time staff members were appointed: Brother Mayer was succeeded by Terry Dold, Richard Bird, Mike Roethle, John Davis, Barry Champion and the present director, Faith Lyons.

Hartland Publications has grown from less than twenty thousand dollars annual operation to an operation of hundreds of thousands of dollars each year. Its goal is to publish truth-filled literature and supplement it by other valuable literature so that God's precious truth can be distributed worldwide. The literature has now spread to scores of countries of the world.

Because of the dilution of the Seventh-day Adventist message in publications from Seventh-day Adventist presses and the huge increase of unsuitable literature available, Hartland Publications has for many people been their number one Christian book store. It is a solemn responsibility for the administration and staff of Hartland Publications to keep placing before the people truth-filled literature. At first a significant number of Adventist Book Centers stocked Hartland Publications' books. Now that avenue of distribution has been greatly reduced because of denominational policies not favorable to selling Hartland-published books. The denominational decision has caused Hartland staff deep sorrow, for it is known that many people find it difficult to obtain these books, especially if they are not in touch with Hartland Institute.

On one occasion a leader from the Review and Herald Publishing Association chanced upon a display of our books at a major gathering of Seventh-day Adventists. She was greatly impressed with the quality and range of the material published by Hartland Publications and wondered why they were not available in regular Seventh-day Adventist outlets. She purchased three hundred dollars worth of our publications and the next day brought her mother, who in turn purchased another fifty dollars worth of books. Here was an example of a woman, unaware of Hartland Publications books, valuing their content when she chanced to see them. It is time for Adventist Book Centers to stock these books.

Hartland Publications is not limited to publishing books. It began publishing a youth magazine produced by students called *Your Choice*. Eventually, as the students were unable to continue its publication, Betsy

Mayer took over the managing editorship of *Your Choice* and transformed it into one of the finest missionary magazines in the Seventh-day Adventist ranks, titled *Last Generation*. This magazine has been responsible for hundreds, possibly thousands of souls around the world accepting the Seventh-day Adventist message. I personally have had the privilege of baptizing a number of these people. One such convert, Helga Zuck, who was baptized at a Hartland camp meeting with her husband, Sam, subsequently became a Board member of Hartland Institute before her untimely death in 2002.

Later, under the leadership and initiative of Janet Evert, *Young Disciple*, a weekly magazine for children and youth ten to sixteen years of age, was launched by Hartland Institute. The magazine is now published in northeastern Washington State where Janet Evert, assisted by her family and other staff, is still the editor. This is, in my judgment, the premier youth magazine in the English speaking world, and has been a great blessing to parents seeking to provide the best spiritual material for their children. Quite a few youth have been led to the Lord by this fine magazine.

Before these publications were established, under the initiative of Elder Milo Sawvel, and edited by Dr. Ted Wade, the Ellen G. White Sabbath School Lesson Comments were published quarterly by Hartland Institute, commencing in 1984. Dr Wade had first approached the Pacific Press and the Review and Herald, inviting them to publish these Spirit of Prophecy comments, but both decided against publishing the material, expressing uncertainty concerning the profitability of such a project. However, later the Pacific Press, no doubt alerted by the Adventist Book Centers to the strong demand for this publication, began publishing their own version of this quarterly. Yet there is still a worldwide demand for the Hartland Ellen G. White *Sabbath School Comments* which has powerful comments in each quarterly. Every day for each quarter, inspired statements are printed in connection with each day's Sabbath School lessons.

The *E. G. White Sabbath School Comments* are now being published under the editorship of Charles and Delpha Tompkins in Northern California. This publication became necessary when in the 1970s the Sabbath School lessons radically changed their format. For many decades the lessons of the *Sabbath School Quarterly* followed a format in which questions were asked, followed by Bible references which, when read, provided the answers to the questions. Then would follow a Spirit of Prophecy comment which would illuminate further the question posed.

However, as I understand it, under increasing pressure, mainly from European Seventh-day Adventist leaders, most of the Spirit of Prophecy material was eliminated, substituted by the comments of the editors and quotations from uninspired authors, many not of our faith. It was claimed that much of the Spirit of Prophecy was not available in continental European languages and therefore should not be featured in the lesson quarterly. If this was true it provided an even greater motivation to retain the Spirit of Prophecy material in the quarterly.

Hartland Publications produces a wide range of audio, video and CD sermons by powerful preachers past and present. It also has produced an outstanding Reformation History CD-ROM, a Nutritional CD-ROM, and music tapes and CDs. Many more important projects are planned for the future. Recognizing the changing times, Hartland Media Center is modernizing its equipment to meet the rapidly increasing demands for CDs and DVDs as the market for audio and video tapes declines.

In the meantime Hartland Publications has expanded widely beyond the Seventh-day Adventist market. Hartland-published books have been sold by the large Christian book distributors. They are stocked by such retailers as Barnes and Noble and are carried by Amazon.com. Also book stores in Great Britain and in Australia stock Hartland Publications books. In this way some of the special books which have been written for the general public are able to be scattered. God has even greater goals for Hartland Publications. These include a great expansion into small outreach booklets and tracts and foreign language literature. Already some Hartland books have been published in Spanish, Portuguese, German, Korean, Bulgarian and Czech.

Just as the medical missionary work will be the last work which can be accomplished for the Lord, the literature and the media will play a central role in the proclamation of the gospel just prior to the close of probation.

# 17    The World Mission

*And they went forth, and preached every where, the Lord working*
*with them, and confirming the word with signs following.*
                                           —Mark 16:20

WHILE the initial missionary outreach efforts of Hartland were primarily confined to the local community, there was always a burning desire that the ministry would develop worldwide. First, however, we deemed it necessary to expand our ministry in the United States. To accomplish this goal God enlisted a very cooperative pastor, Elder James Wolter, together with his wife, Doris, who were dedicated to present truth and the faithful presentation of the three angels' messages. While at Weimar Institute I had preached a number of times in Elder Wolter's church and realized the dedication of this couple. He was pastoring the Ontario Church in California at the time. When it was decided to hold Hartland Bible Conferences (first called Our Firm Foundation Conferences) in various parts of the United States, Elder Wolter was delighted to host the first one during the latter part of December 1983, less than six months after Hartland Institute had been established.

The late Pastor George Burnside, the Spirit-filled New Zealand evangelist, came from Australia for the series. Elder Leo Van Dolson from the Sabbath School Department of the General Conference also participated. Elder Tom Davis, from the Review and Herald Publishing Association, and his wife, Margaret, spoke. Elders Robert Wieland and Donald Short made presentations. Dr. Leroy Moore, Director of Native American work of the General Conference; Elder Ron Spear, revivalist; Elder John Stevens, Religious Liberty Director of the Pacific Union; Pastor Alex Snyman, Huntington Park Seventh-day Adventist Church pastor; and Pastor Robert Taylor, Sacramento Woodside Seventh-day Adventist Church all participated. From Hartland Institute, speakers included Elder Milo Sawvel, Pastor David Grams, Dr. Warren Peters and me. More than six hundred people participated in the initial conference.

A succession of such conferences was held over the next few years. These conferences were held in Hendersonville and Arden, North Carolina; Marietta, Georgia; Ontario, California; Chula Vista (San Diego),

California; Gentry, Arkansas; Brunswick, Maine; Woodland (Sacramento), California; Central Orlando, Florida; and Witley in England. Concurrently Hartland speakers, including myself, were travelling to many churches bringing the urgent message of the hour to God's people. At this time I had the privilege to preach at Conference camp meetings—the Central camp meeting of the Texas Conference held at Nameless Valley Ranch, and also the Ottawa camp meeting for the Ontario Conference in Canada.

Unfortunately some who spoke in our earliest convocations and Bible Conferences have publicly moved away from the biblical truths espoused by Hartland. It has been our goal to separate peaceably in such circumstances while yet warning our listeners and readers of the errors being proclaimed. This has proven a difficult balancing act, not always easy to achieve.

Our first overseas Hartland Bible Conference was held in Witley, a small village in the county of Surrey in England. My brother Russell was then Medical Director of Enton Medical Centre in Surrey and he eagerly sought to host such a conference there. He had worked very closely with the president of the South England Conference who had agreed to make the New Gallery Center in Regent Street in the heart of London available for the Bible conference. Sadly at the last moment, the venue was cancelled as the President came under great pressure from a group of the white pastors in the South England Conference. The excuse seized upon for the late cancellation of the use of this promised venue did not, of course, reveal the correct reason. Letters had been sent to church pastors in South England requesting them to apprise their congregations of this special meeting. The then president of the South England Conference cited this as his "reason" to breach his promise. This president had known me well when I was the West Indies College president in Jamaica and he was president of the West Jamaica Conference. We had shared cordial relations at that time.

This cancellation was to set a precedent. In Australia and the United States we had booked denominational venues for meetings by Hartland, only at a later stage to find them cancelled, thus causing great difficulties. One such cancellation was at the behest of the South Queensland Conference in Australia, the other meeting was cancelled by Atlantic Union College in the United States. I must state that, by contrast, not one venue promised by a non-Seventh-day Adventist denomination has ever cancelled a booking.

The venue was transferred to a hall in the Surrey village of Witley where the conference was held. The speakers were confined to three—

Dr. Russell Standish, Dr. Robert Dunn and me. Quite an array of people came from far and wide, approximately two hundred in all, in spite of the last minute change of venue. This was to lead to conferences being held later in the Coventry Church in the Midlands of England and the first Gazeley meetings in the Old Anglican Rectory in East Anglia. But more of this will be described later.

Hartland speakers traveled far and wide earnestly seeking to enlighten and warn God's people of the perilous times in which we now live. Not always was our presence welcome. But as in the times of Christ many of the "common" people heard us gladly. As the time approached for the 1985 General Conference in New Orleans, Louisiana, Hartland applied for and was granted permission to set up a booth during the ministerial pre-session prior to the commencement of the General Conference session. A special display board was prepared to illustrate the educational and health emphasis of our Institute. Its major theme was depicted as "A World Vision." At the time this display board was prepared the only overseas meetings which had been held were the Witley meetings in England. Yet the theme reflected the cherished world vision to proclaim the present truth gospel to the world. At that time no World Mission Division existed. The establishment of that Division had to wait until the beginning of the 1990s when Hal Mayer became the first Director of the World Mission Division. In the meantime Hartland's ministry was rapidly expanding both locally and overseas. Brother Mayer was succeeded by Laura Lickey, Jeff Wehr and the Present Director Frances Lundberg.

In 1986 Hartland Bible Conference revisited England again and extended its overseas outreach to Australia, New Zealand and the Netherlands. In 1987 we traveled to England, the Netherlands, Belgium, France and Italy, presenting truth-filled messages and Hartland Bible Conferences. As of 2002 Hartland's staff and students have ministered in ninety-eight countries. Public evangelistic meetings have also been held in many countries. Extension schools have been held in Zimbabwe, Ghana, Nigeria, Kenya, India, Fiji, Papua New Guinea, Cameroon, Zambia, and Romania. On every inhabited continent many precious souls have been added to God's kingdom and the Seventh-day Adventist church through the ministry of Hartland Institute. Yet there are many more nations which need the saving truths of the gospel. All the inhabitants of the earth will hear the mighty call, "Come out of her, my people" (Revelation 18:4).

Hartland World Mission has spread the word through tens of millions of pages of literature to far-flung corners of the planet. It has been responsible for placing the *Great Controversy* on the web site in thirteen different major languages of the world. The World Mission Division has been responsible for health ministry outreach conducted in many places around the earth.

Beyond its focused role to bring the gospel to overseas nations, the World Mission Division is responsible for Hartland's annual camp meeting. The first Hartland camp meeting was held in August, 1988, and it has been held every year since, usually from the end of July to early August. So successful were the camp meetings that World Mission was urged to commence meetings between the annual camp meetings. Convocations in the fall, winter and spring are now an important part of Hartland's regular calendar. The first of these convocations was held in 1990.

Until our present pavilion was built in 1993, a very large hired tent was pitched on our campus near the mansion. It was rented with many hundreds of chairs for the attendees. Prior to the building of the heated pavilion, the winters were too cold to hold a winter convocation and for three years they were held in Maryland in the greater Washington, D.C. area. By the grace of God and the generosity of His people, Hartland was able to build a commodious pavilion which can hold at least one thousand people. The pavilion was so constructed that a major section of it can be enclosed and heated for the fall, winter and spring convocations. The attendance is such that on some occasions not everyone can be seated in the pavilion during the Sabbath divine service at the fall and spring convocations. However we have been able to make arrangements for the overflow to participate through video monitors. The enclosed portion of the pavilion is soon to be enlarged.

It is also the responsibility of the Hartland World Mission Division to arrange Hartland camp meetings within North America and speaking appointments for some of the many speakers who regularly are invited to preach in different locations. With a small staff, Hartland World Mission nevertheless does a mighty work for the cause of the gospel and contributes very significantly to the mission of the Institute, playing a pivotal role in the continued expansion of the worldwide ministry.

# 18    The Stewardship Division

*But this I say, He which soweth sparingly shall reap also sparingly; and he which soweth bountifully shall reap also bountifully.*        —2 Corinthians 9:6-8

THE Stewardship Division is a recent addition to the ministry of Hartland. However, some aspects of the stewardship ministry have been with Hartland since before it was founded. More recently the role of the stewardship ministry has broadened greatly.

At the beginning of Hartland Institute, Elder Milo Sawvel was asked to be the inaugural Development Director. It was through his very energetic efforts, blessed by the Holy Spirit, that many of the urgent, time-sensitive financial goals of Hartland were met. It is one of the greatest miracles wrought by God that Hartland Institute never missed a deadline for major financial obligations. Neither, because of the blessing of the Lord, has Hartland missed a payroll for the staff. There were times when it appeared almost certain that staff stipends would be missed or significantly delayed. But every time, prayer solved the dilemma. The Scriptures says,

The effectual fervent prayer of a righteous man availeth much.
—James 5:16

How much more is God's power displayed when a whole body of united believers pray earnestly for the Lord to intervene in difficulties. There was one occasion when we feared the finances were so dangerously low that we seriously considered reducing the small stipends that the staff members were receiving. Once again God made it plain that He was in charge of the finances.

. . . There is a God in heaven.        —Daniel 2:28

Three successive men led the development division in its first decade. Elder Sawvel was succeeded by the late Richard Gister who in turn was succeeded by Ron Goss. All worked diligently to help provide for the multifaceted needs of a diverse institute as it developed its ministries. There followed a seven-year period when there was no Development Director. Some felt that the financial support of the friends of the institute would diminish significantly with the lack of a development leader. We faced a level of uncertainty. Yet most of us realized that Hartland is not man's institution, it is God's. If we were faithful to Him and earnestly sought His leadership all would work to His glory. It was a wonderful exercise in training the division leaders to be responsible with God for raising the funds for their divisions. Now they had to take the major responsibility for the needs of their divisions and for encouraging the support of the many worthy projects of a ministry so diverse as Hartland. To the amazement of all, the support to Hartland remained steady with no evidence of decline. Each division leader took seriously his or her role to encourage support for the division's ministries and that continues to be a blessing today.

However, in the year 2000 it was voted by the Board of Directors on the recommendation of the Administrative Committee to establish a fifth division of Hartland—the Stewardship Ministry Division. Brother Hal Mayer was named the Director of this Division. The responsibilities had been significantly broadened because we recognized that stewardship extends far beyond simply financial solicitation. At its center is the salvation of souls, for it is in the realm of stewardship that our dedication and love for God is best expressed. It first and foremost focuses upon the stewardship of our hearts and minds. The Scripture says, "Where your treasure is, there will your heart be also" (Luke 12:34). Where our heart is, is the key to salvation. The heart is symbolic of the mind. It includes the talent of time, especially our discretionary time. How we employ our discretionary time reflects how closely we are committed to Jesus. If it is spent in idle activities, feverishly following various forms of entertainment, simple socializing or other unproductive pursuits, it is unmistakable evidence that Christ is not dwelling in our hearts. However, if our time is invested in the study of God's Word, in His counsels, in witnessing to others, in caring for the needy and sick and other such profitable activities, then there is evidence of a transformed life, a life of one who is walking in the footsteps of his Maker

Stewardship also includes the way we handle the financial resources which God has entrusted to us. Love for Christ motivates us to support His work. It is this motivation which focuses our minds to overcome greed, selfishness and covetousness. True stewards recognize that every blessing they receive is a gift from God, a resource to be used for His glory, for the progress of His work and for the hastening of the return of our blessed Lord and Savior. They also recognize that He gives to them a measure of responsibility to demonstrate that their gifts and energies are used to support those efforts and ministries which uphold and proclaim the truth.

The goal of the Stewardship Division of Hartland is first, to help men and women to the kingdom of heaven. The Stewardship Department stands ready to help those who are seeking an understanding of a deeper connection with the Lord. The staff in this Division are joyfully willing to help the weary wanderer on his or her journey to the kingdom of heaven. Also following the counsel of the Lord, the Stewardship Division shares the needs of the work which God has given Hartland to accomplish. While some of the needs are necessary to maintain or upgrade the facilities on the campus, yet most of the needs are for the ministry which God has placed before us. Hartland's goals are largely to fulfill the soul-winning ministry which God has assigned.

The staff of Hartland thank God for the faithful donors and volunteers whose self-sacrificing gifts and services have been responsible for the repairs and the refurbishing of the mansion, the construction and equipping of Hartland Wellness Center, for Hartland College administration, Hartland Publications, the pavilion, and still more recently the shower facilities for those who attend the convocations, conventions and camp meetings which are conducted at Hartland Institute. They also thank God for those who have been so generous with their gifts to help build homes on campus to ease the financial burden of renting homes off campus. It has been faithful and generous supporters who have paved the roads, constructed student dormitories, fenced around the gardens to protect from the deer, and built greenhouses.

However the ministry focus is dominant. Hartland donors have been responsible for large quantities of soul-winning literature sent around the world, which has resulted in many hundreds now rejoicing in the Sabbath and the three angels' messages. This could only have been possible because of the large and generous support for free literature from faithful and committed men and women who love the truth and love souls. The friends of Hartland have wonderfully supported the missionary training fund which is employed to train mainly foreign students who have no other way of obtaining the true education which Hartland offers, so that they too might be part of the final generation to take the gospel to the world. It is these generous and self-sacrificing friends of Hartland who help with evangelism, extension schools, health ministry outreach and a multitude of other aspects of ministry. It has been these wonderful people who have helped raise funds for desperately needy individuals to receive the blessing of restored health at Hartland Wellness Center. These supporters have even helped newly established institutions, some started by our graduates, former staff members and by other faithful workers. Those funds have helped establish radio stations and television outreach in foreign countries, and provided simple vehicles and materials for dedicated local missionaries who are focused upon the spread of the gospel in these far-flung places throughout the world.

Without these many faithful supporters and faith partners there is no way that Hartland could do the vast-ranging ministry for which it is known. It is the Stewardship Ministry Division which seeks to nurture the souls of those who are in need and to offer the God-appointed opportunities to help forward the missionary work of Hartland. Together Hartland and its partners face the final challenge to receive the fullness of the power of the latter rain which alone will accomplish the gospel completion as the final saving invitation of Christ will reach every inhabitant of the planet.

# 19     The Home Schoolers

*Train up a child in the way he should go: and when he is old, he will not depart from it.*           —Proverbs 22:6

WHEN Hartland began there were no laws in Virginia to permit the home schooling of children. This was causing deep anxiety as many parents were convicted that the public schools and even many of the parochial schools were not safe places for their children to be educated. Some parents were in hiding; others were under investigation. There were some parents who were facing prosecution. However there was a strong ground swell in Virginia for the State House to provide legislation which would permit responsible parents to home school their children.

We were too new to Virginia to understand what had been taking place. However, one morning, early in 1984, as I was sitting in my office, I received a phone call from a woman I had met once or twice but did not know well at that time. She asked why I was not in Richmond to give testimony before the committee of delegates and senators who were holding hearings from concerned citizens on the issue of home schooling. I asked when the meeting was taking place. She responded, "At ten o'clock today!" Hartland is nearly two hours drive from Richmond and it was then about nine o'clock in the morning, I told her it was not possible to arrive for the start of the meeting but I would attend, leaving immediately, in the hope that it would be possible for me to give testimony.

I asked Brother Mayer to accompany me and we quickly left Hartland, arriving at the meeting about eleven o'clock. There was a list where anyone who desired to give testimony could sign up. I noted that my signature was number fifty-seven. I realized that already number twenty-three was speaking. As we sat down we had the opportunity to gage the concerns—often very emotional concerns—of those who were giving testimony before the joint committee of Delegates and Senators. Some of those giving testimony expressed a good deal of anger against the State House, which I thought counterproductive. Others said they were representing home-schooling parents who were afraid to attend the meeting for fear of identification by officials. However most, whether calm or emotional, gave very similar statements. I realized that it would be wise to present something different when my turn arrived. Each individual was given two minutes speaking time. I asked the Lord for guidance as to what I could say in two minutes that would make a difference.

Eventually number fifty-seven was called and I moved quickly to the microphone. There was no time for an introduction or for any elaborations. This was my submission,

> My name is Colin Standish. I am the President of Hartland College in Rapidan, Virginia. We commenced September last year. We had checked many of the states along the eastern seaboard of the United States desiring to operate as a religiously exempt college. Only in Virginia was there such an option. Thank the Lord for Thomas Jefferson!
>
> Today we are asking the State House to establish legislation which will permit the same freedom to parents of elementary and secondary students to be able to operate an educational program for their children as Hartland College enjoys without the interference of the State. Today we have the opportunity to decide whether we will follow the Greek pagan concept of education or the Judeo-Christian concept of education. The Judeo-Christian concept of education, built upon Holy Scripture, declares that the parents have the prerogatives in education. By contrast the pagans held that the State had the prerogatives in the education of the children. That has been the claim of every totalitarian state that has arisen, including Nazi Germany and Communist Soviet Union. I trust that the State House will follow the Judeo-Christian concepts providing parents the opportunity to choose to home school their children responsibly.

Before I was able to resume my seat one of the committee members asked me from where I came originally. No doubt he noted my accent. I answered "Australia." He asked no other question. I suspected that he was not favorable to the home-school bill and that he believed I was from Great Britain. He probably believed that Great Britain, as an old-world traditionalist nation, was very resistant to the home-schooling movement. He probably thought that Australia, being a new world country, would have been more open to home schooling. In reality it was the other way around. Great Britain is quite open to home schooling. Australia is quite restrictive.

The only speaker to follow me was the very woman who had alerted me to the meeting at the State House. Ironically she was the only Afro-American to speak. She created lightness to the meeting by saying she wanted to "add a little color to the proceedings." When the proceedings concluded, a delegate and a senator came to talk with me and invite me to their offices. The senator was a high-profile Republican who shortly thereafter, unsuccessfully, ran for Lieutenant-Governor. Both men desired my counsel as to how to proceed because both were favorable to a home-school bill. Both indicated that they believed that they could get a bill passed in the House but it was going to be very difficult to succeed in the Senate. The senator asked me to help him decide what issues were nonnegotiable for a good home-school bill. We spent quite some time together and I believe it helped him to make those decisions. The senator said he would legislate no restrictions as he believed home-school parents generally provided better education than public schools, but he knew that such a bill would certainly fail.

We learned that a week later the State Board of Education was to meet to decide what their recommendation would be to the State House. Brother Mayer and I decided that it was essential to be there for that meeting also. This time we arrived early, giving us an opportunity to review the *Richmond Times Dispatch*. Their editorial stated it was unlikely that the State Board of Education would recommend any kind of a home-school bill to the State House, and that their recommendation would be very important to the final outcome of the vote in the House of Delegates and the Senate.

We were quite surprised to find that only four people had arrived to give testimony. It was as if the public did not know the importance of this meeting. The first two citizens to testify gave rather emotional appeals. However, I was most impressed with Mary Kay Clark. Mary Kay was a Roman Catholic—one of the four women co-leaders of the Home Educator's Association of Virginia. She was a woman with great understanding of the issues and we had the opportunity to speak together at some length. She herself had been principal of a Roman Catholic high school but had become disillusioned when the Roman Catholic schools moved away from their distinctive curriculum, following mainly the same curriculum and text books as the state schools. Mary Kay had sent her children to a Seventh-day Adventist school but was disappointed with the atmosphere of the school. She had also investigated the curriculum of a Seventh-day Adventist educational institution of higher learning. She asked me a very difficult question. Why is your curriculum not more Seventh-day Adventist? She shared with me her curriculum in English. Of course it would not be that which Seventh-day Adventists would recommend. However, it showed she had the right idea. In her curriculum, instead of reading novels and drama she recommended for literature the study of the lives of the saints and the papal encyclicals.

I was the last of the four to give testimony and I repeated the speech which I had made before the ad hoc committee of delegates and senators. All that we could do then was listen to the dialogue back and forth by the nine members of the Virginia State Board of Education. It was clear from the dialogue that it would not be a unanimous vote either way. However, it was hard to determine what the outcome would be. We were surprised to hear some of the members speaking very favorably toward a home-school bill and ultimately, by a vote of six to three, they voted to recommend that a responsible home-school bill be prepared by the House of Delegates and the Senate. Ultimately a good home-school bill was voted, giving the freedom to parents to educate their children according to the dictates of their consciences.

We were thankful to have a little part to play in helping forward such a bill. The influence of Hartland did not stop there. One of our students from Montana, Nanette Christensen, learning that the State House in Montana was considering a restrictive home-school bill, decided that she would make an appeal at the State House. At the time Montana had the most open home-school situation in America. The government declared it had responsibility for public education only and therefore parents were given full freedom to undertake home schooling. At the hearing Nanette made a wonderful speech which later I heard on audio tape. She pointed out that she had traveled all the way to Virginia to obtain the kind of education which she desired and she urged that all the citizens of Montana would continue to have the freedom to operate home schools should they so choose, so that their children would not have to leave the state. There was no question that her presentation made a profound impact, indeed to such an extent that no changes were made in the law.

Today Hartland Institute still has a strong interest in home schooling. Many of the parents on our campus home school their children. Hartland Publications carries an array of books which are helpful to home-schooling parents and she, from time to time, travels to assist in presentations to home-school parents.

# 20 The Ministry Expansion

*Go ye therefore, and teach all nations, baptizing them in the name of the Father, and of the Son, and of the Holy Ghost: teaching them to observe all things whatsoever I have commanded you: and, lo, I am with you alway, even unto the end of the world.*
—Matthew 28:19, 20

EARLY in the experience of Hartland Institute the vision of the staff was increasingly focused upon presenting the gospel widely. The completion of the gospel commission burns brightly in the hearts of the staff. We felt compelled by the Holy Spirit to exert every energy in this endeavor. Hartland staff responded earnestly to the call of Sister White to work for

. . . the purifying of the church and the warning of the world.
—*Testimonies*, Vol. 5, p. 187

Thus the expansion of its ministry was within the church and to the world.

Frequently in the initial years of Hartland's development there was criticism that self-supporting ministries were focused upon inreach and not outreach. Even in these early days, that inaccurate assessment was designed to discredit the earnest endeavors of faithful self-supporting institutions. However, it is always necessary to establish strong foundations for a new institution, and the administration of Hartland wisely decided that unless the focus and philosophy were well-defined and unified, unless the facilities were adequate and the quality of the staff strong, the institution would ever be imperiled, or at most it would struggle along with unclear and dubious mission and unreliable financial support. If the history of self-supporting institutions is surveyed it will be noted that many institutions which began with great enthusiasm, earnestness and hope have been closed within a few years; others have limped along with little fruit for their sacrificial efforts. Cognizance of these facts led us to a diligent study of God's counsels, determined that we would trust them and follow each one.

We identified a number of reasons for the failure of self-supporting ministries. Frequently those beginning a self-supporting work are willing to take anyone who offers his or her service regardless of their skills, motivation, or even their spiritual maturity. This course is perilous to the success of the organization. Others give little attention to establishing a sound financial basis. Even the most sacrificial effort cannot long sustain an institution without a viable staff of dedicated Seventh-day Adventists well educated in the principles of God's service and possessing a thorough knowledge of sound financial planning. Shoes and clothing wear out, vehicles deteriorate, personal resources deplete, and thus terrible stress is placed upon both staff and institution. Valuable staff are forced to leave and suitable replacements are not always easy to attract. Filling positions with incompetent or ineffective individuals only exacerbates the problem and brings discredit upon the organization. Often those who have counterproductive personal goals are permitted to connect with the institution. There is not always a careful investigation of references, beliefs, character and Christian practices before such applicants are hastily added to the staff. Winds of doctrine and schisms arise, and the stability of the institution is greatly compromised.

There are further issues which lead to the failure of self-supporting ministries. Often the leader has a vision but has little experience in leadership or successful administration. Lacking such skills at the head, the institution is certain to flounder and this jeopardizes its future. Institutional leadership has to learn how to generate income. It is not sufficient to rely upon donations for the operation of the institution. The counsel of the Lord is that the operational costs should be generated by the institution's own activities.

> In some of our schools the price of tuitions has been too low. This has in many ways been detrimental to the educational work. . . . Whatever may have been the object in placing the tuition at less than a living rate, the fact that a school has been running behind heavily is sufficient reason for reconsidering the plans and arranging its charges so that in the future its showing may be different. The amount charged for tuition, board, and residence should be sufficient to pay the salaries of the faculty, to supply the table with an abundance of healthful, nourishing food, to maintain the furnishing of the rooms, to keep the buildings in repair, and to meet other necessary running expenses [operational costs].
> —*Testimonies*, Vol. 6, 210, 211

In other words, Sister White advocated that operational costs should be covered by tuition.

> The churches in different localities should feel that a solemn responsibility rests upon them to train youth and educate talent to engage in missionary work. When they see those in the church who give promise

of making useful workers, but who are not able to support themselves in the school, they should assume the responsibility of sending them to one of our training schools. . . . There are persons who would do good service in the Lord's vineyard, but many are too poor to obtain without assistance the education that they require.     —*Ibid.*, 211

Donations must be reserved largely for major capital development and the spread of the gospel. Many self-supporting institutions do not pay due regard to such matters. The leaders assume that the Lord will sustain them. Some also have little understanding of how to generate support for their institution and, though sacrifice is great, nevertheless the institution flounders and frequently ends in failure.

Thus securing the ministry on firm and solid principles is essential to a newly established institution. However, a developing institution cannot place all its resources and efforts into maintaining the institution. Rather it must reach out in ministry to the church, to the community and to the world at large. Otherwise it has no valid justification for existence.

From the very beginning there was a burning passion in the hearts of most of those who had established Hartland Institute to seek and save the lost, to be a blessing to the church and to focus upon soul-winning in the world. The first efforts in ministry targeted outreach in the local communities. Souls were soon led to the Lord. One of the most blessed early experiences was in the conversion of a young Mennonite woman, Edna Martin. Edna, a delightful woman, tragically had the dread disease of cancer. It was in an advanced state when she arrived at Hartland. She spent much time at Hartland seeking assistance from the Wellness Center, but also, with her beautiful personality she was reaching out to other health guests. Despite following all of God's healing methods Edna eventually succumbed to the cancer and passed to an untimely death. We look to the blessed resurrection day and by God's grace we will see her again. God's health principles had greatly increased the quality of her life and extended it beyond that estimated by her physician. Two years prior to her death Edna accepted the precious Seventh-day Adventist truth and was baptized.

Crusades were run by staff and students, each one having its impact in souls for the kingdom. The first major overseas evangelistic efforts were conducted by senior students in Tanzania in 1989. Student evangelists included Ray De Carlo, Lynwood Spangler and Scott Schafer. It was thrilling to watch as each one of these men led many souls to the Seventh-day Adventist faith and to the kingdom of heaven.

Soon evangelism went forth to every continent of the world and in many nations. It would be impossible to approximate the number who have accepted the three angels' messages and become part of God's church. However, when it became plain that institutions such as Hartland were vigorous in outreach, there was not praise and thankfulness from many denominational leaders. The only difference noted was that now there were no longer claims that self-supporting work concentrated on inreach and not on outreach. Rather now the criticism was that they were holding these meetings without proper authorization from duly constituted authorities. All this, to say the least, was perplexing. It gave rise to the suspicion that the first criticism, which seemed to urge outreach by self-supporting institutions, was far less sincere than it first appeared. And too, this cry that our evangelistic endeavors were not approved by properly constituted church authority fell far short of credibility because of the persistent refusal of our church organizations to cooperate with Hartland's earnest soul-winning efforts. It was the church leaders, seemingly indifferent to souls, who through the Holy Spirit we had brought to the kingdom of heaven, who withheld cooperation. Surely God desires His faithful servants to work together in unity to accomplish the goals of the gospel commission in a cooperative and non-controlling atmosphere..

Other criticisms dealt with claims that self-supporting pastors did not supply the full services of a denominational pastor. Yet once again the validity of such claims was questionable. Hartland Institute and other similar institutions have spent much time in care and ministry to the sick, in seeking to help the spiritually weakened and backslidden. Hartland staff and students have been successful in reclaiming some of these for the kingdom of heaven. Further, Hartland pastors have the privilege of performing weddings, baby dedications, funerals, communion services, anointings of the sick and baptisms. When it became clear that self-supporting ministers were effectively fulfilling the entire role of ministry, there should have been expressions of satisfaction by many denominational leaders. This should have been especially true of baptisms, as in many cases those baptized were accepted into the fellowship of faithful Seventh-day Adventist denominational churches. But this was not to be. Now the concern over our work shifted again. The criticism was now raised that ministerial functions were being conducted without Conference authority, though most often these services were undertaken by ordained self-supporting workers. We were left with the irrefutable conclusion that many in denomination ministry were determined to denigrate our work irrespective of the fact that we undertook our work in harmony with Scripture and the Spirit of Prophecy.

It became increasingly important for Hartland to do the ministry that God had called it to fulfill without regard to criticism or opposition or the rumors promulgated by some Conference leaders. It would seem that there was no way that self-supporting workers could satisfy both the Lord and our denominational church leaders. We were greatly saddened by this. Unless our work was subject to the human leader's control and authority it would never be approved. Thus we had to choose between the call of God and the authority of man. We uncompromisingly chose the former.

Of course there are those who hasten to point out that some "supporting ministries" work very faithfully with "the church." Hartland does not condemn the concessions that such ministries have made, if they truly believe that this is what God has called them to do. But Hartland's study of the Bible and the Spirit of Prophecy has not supported making such limiting concessions. Hartland is committed to obeying God rather than man. Yet this divine injunction has never been used by Hartland to be less than cooperative to the fullest extent with other Seventh-day Adventists when such cooperation breaches no divine directive.

Many times the self-supporting workers of the past have had to continue a ministry in face of the fierce opposition of denominational leaders. One has only to review the ministry of men such as Elijah, Isaiah, Jeremiah and John the Baptist; or, in the Christian era, the apostles, Celts, Waldensians, Huguenots and Albigenses, to find similar precedents. God's church throughout the ages has found great difficulty in learning the lessons from evil examples of generations which have passed before.

Even in the Seventh-day Adventist church, in spite of the support of Sister White, men such as E. A. Sutherland and Percy Magan, who were founders of the self-supporting Madison School, faced fierce opposition and inappropriate restrictions from the leaders of their day. Above all the pattern of our Savior exemplifies the necessity of doing our Father's will in the face of unsanctified control exerted by leaders.

Every successful self-supporting ministry will be established on the principles of God's Word. It will be focused upon ministering to God's chosen people and to the world at large. Its personnel will be wholly dedicated to God and therefore will be loyal to His church. It will support God's remnant church but not the apostasy, worldliness and wickedness so prevalent in the church. Indeed, in great love and with a sincere burden resting in our hearts, its ministry will act as a sentinel to warn against the inroads of Satan and to bring to God's people the light and truth of the everlasting gospel.

# 21    The Crisis

*And Barnabas determined to take with them John, whose sur-
name was Mark. But Paul thought not good to take him with
them, who departed from them from Pamphylia, and went not with
them to the work. And the contention was so sharp between them,
that they departed asunder one from the other: and so Barnabas
took Mark, and sailed unto Cyprus*          —Acts 15:37-39

AT the staff colloquium held prior to the beginning of the 1987–88 school year I made a statement to the staff, "We are approaching the fifth year of the life of Hartland Institute. Experts have claimed that the fifth year is frequently the danger year for new organizations." In the early days of any new organization there is a level of euphoria and camaraderie as the new organization is pioneered. This develops a strong cohesiveness and the inevitable struggles bind staff members together. This phenomenon is apparent not only in Christian organizations, but also in secular organizations, businesses and corporations. However, with the passage of time it becomes apparent that different goals, different perceptions of mission, and selfish ambitions become evident. Those matters which were not evident or were not considered important, begin to take on a greater magnitude in the attitudes and perceptions of the members of the team. Ultimately about the fifth year this frequently leads to acrimonious divisions. I urged the staff not to permit this to happen at Hartland. But beyond all my worst forebodings it did.

It is accurate for me to say that in all my more than fifty-year ministry for the Lord, this was by far the greatest test and trial of my life. It tested my faith, my courage, my strength and my trust. Hartland Institute was shaken to its very foundation. It appeared that the institution was about to take a U-turn in its direction. There were times when I despaired. It seemed that all the forces of hell were let loose on the campus. Only God knows how it began: He alone was able to spare the ministry of Hartland.

The first inkling I had came in February of 1988 when we were conducting a Hartland Bible Conference at the Chula Vista Church, San

Diego in the Southeastern California Conference. In a casual walk with the publishing director of Hope International, Brother Henry Cowan, I was informed that there was rebellion on Hartland's campus. This, to a significant degree, was surprising as I was not aware of it; so I pressed Brother Cowan for names. They were withheld on the basis that he had been pledged to secrecy. However I was given to understand there were two ringleaders.

As I contemplated the words of this man I identified two men on the staff whom I believed could be responsible. Later my deductions proved correct. One was a Bible teacher in the College and the other a physician in the Health Center (now called the Wellness Center). My mind reflected upon the beginning of 1988. The Bible teacher had come to my office very agitated, demanding that we sever all connection with Hope International. I asked him upon what grounds he was demanding this. He told me that Hope was calling people to leave the Seventh-day Adventist Church and it had divided many churches around America. My response was simply, "If that is true then certainly we will separate from Hope International no matter how much I appreciate Ron Spear as a friend." But I added, "I have not found any evidence of it. However if you have evidence, place it before me." Quite aggressively the Bible teacher responded, "I will get you all the evidence you need." Some days later that same staff member returned with a twenty-eight page document, dropped it on my desk and he left with the words, "There is all the evidence you need."

I read through the document carefully searching for the evidence. I found not one shred of evidence in all the twenty-eight pages. What I found was a barrage of accusations against Hope International, Elder Ron Spear, and *Our Firm Foundation* magazine, from various church administrators and leaders and, sadly, even some self-supporting workers. Two days later the staff member returned. Still evidencing the same aggressive spirit, he asked me, "Well, what did you think of what I gave you?" Calling him by name, I responded, "I asked you for evidence. All I have here is twenty-eight pages of accusations." My response obviously angered the staff member, and no doubt I too was exercised more than I should have been. The staff member retorted, "Those statements come from General Conference, Division, Union and local Conference leaders." I replied, "I do not care whether they come from the angel Gabriel, I asked you for evidence and all you have given is accusations." He continued, "Well, what did you want for evidence?" "I expected the names of churches which could be verified as having been divided by the ministry of Hope International. I looked for evidence of people who stated that they withdrew their membership from the Seventh-day Adventist Church because of the ministry of Hope International. I found not one cited in the twenty-eight page document," I said.

Clearly my unwillingness to accept accusations and rumors as of equal value with evidence caused a deep seething in the heart of this Bible teacher. I had underestimated the intensity of his response and his determined efforts which would follow to do all in his power to separate Hartland from ministering with Hope International. Understandably, I began to suspect that this staff member was one of the unidentified "rebel" leaders.

It was a little different with the doctor, whom I found to be not an easy man with whom to labor. He also caused considerable heartache for Dr. Warren Peters and the health team. There were other issues. Though he had a very nice family they did not uphold some of the Bible and Spirit of Prophecy principles concerning dress or student social relations which Hartland Institute espoused on the basis of divine counsel. This had caused us significant difficulty and I believe that a number of students became disaffected with Hartland College, resulting in their departure. I had addressed these issues with the doctor but to no effect. Thus I sensed rightly that he was the other "dissident" leader. However, I wrongly judged that the influence of both men would not be great.

The Bible teacher was well liked but some evaluated his teaching to be disorganized. As far as I knew, he was teaching the true gospel. He had been the Bible teacher for the first two years of Hartland and then left, but had returned after one year of serving elsewhere. Up until this point I had found him to be affable, hard working and cooperative. However I later discovered the reason for the sudden rise of his expressed concerns. He had called the then president of the Michigan Conference to discuss with him the possibility of considering some of our upcoming pastoral evangelism graduates to be called to his conference. The president had responded that he would only consider Hartland graduates if we severed all association with Hope International.

I had seriously underestimated the influence which this Bible teacher would exert upon board members, staff and students. I was fully aware of what I believed were malicious rumors concerning the disloyalty of Hope International and especially its leader, Elder Ron Spear. I knew that there was great antagonism to *Our Firm Foundation* magazine because it was upsetting the comfort zone of many leaders who were not willing to face the reality of the terrible doctrinal apostasy and worldliness that was sweeping into our beloved church. Thus in July of 1988, when the crisis at Hartland had greatly exacerbated, I decided that I would test the validity of the claims that Hope was a divisive organization leading people away from God's remnant church. While I did not believe these claims, I believed I must test them.

I was assigned the responsibility of preaching the Friday evening service at the Hope International camp meeting where about eight hundred people were present. Without revealing my plans to anyone, not even to Elder Spear, I asked a number of questions before preaching my sermon. The only people whom I had alerted were the video operators. I explained that I would be asking some questions and I would be calling for a show of hands at which time the cameras were to focus on the audience so that this response could be recorded on video.

My first question was, "How many of you are members of a local Seventh-day Adventist church?" The hands went up en masse all over the congregation, too numerous to count. My second question was, "How many of you were once members of the Seventh-day Adventist church who have now separated yourself from it?" To my amazement not one hand was raised. I thought that maybe a handful of separationists might have been in the congregation. But that proved not to be the case. Thus I did not ask my third question which would have been, "Did you leave because someone connected with Hope International encouraged you to leave?"

I now proceeded to another line of questions. "How many of you have ever heard a representative of Hope International encourage you to leave the Seventh-day Adventist Church?" Not one hand was raised. Then I asked my final question, "How many of you have ever heard someone associated with Hope International encourage you to stay loyal to the Seventh-day Adventist church." Again the hands were raised en masse around the pavilion. I cannot say that every hand was raised but one fact is certain, it could only have been very few who did not raise their hands. Yet such is the power of false rumors that, when I thought to share these irrefutable and clear facts with leaders in the General Conference and in the Washington Conference, I found no interest whatsoever in the evidence which I had accumulated. Prejudice is very impelling.

Ironically at the very next Hope camp meeting of 1989, as I rose to present the divine service, five people around the pavilion stood up with placards which proclaimed, "Repent, Ron [Spear], Repent, Colin [Standish], Repent, Ty [Gibson] for telling these people to remain faithful to the corrupt Seventh-day Adventist Church." In the intervening years these kinds of false rumors concerning Hope International and Hartland continue. It has always been the testimony of history that those who love God's church enough to warn against the inroads of Satan's nefarious deceptions are seen as the troublers of Israel rather than being seen as a people who truly love God and His church with all their heart and soul and mind.

During the early part of 1988, the conflict was made especially difficult in that I had accepted appointments along with Dr. Peters and Brother Hal Mayer for a three-week itinerary to Thailand, Malaysia and Singapore. There was little I could do in the circumstances except pray. However another complication arose. We were at this time building the Wellness Center. I knew we were running low on funds and the day before I left the treasurer informed me that we had only about eight thousand dollars left in the building fund. I told him that all paid workers on the building project would have to be laid off when funds were depleted until more funds became available. As will be seen later, this had serious repercussion.

The situation exacerbated when, the night before our early morning departure, the business manager explained that he had made a mistake and that actually we were now seven or eight thousand dollars in debt with no cash available. How I wished I could be there the next morning to explain the situation to the workers. But that was impossible and I feared that it would create problems. As I feared, great hostility was generated when the staff of paid workers, who had not been warned in advance, were apprised of the situation. I had already instructed the treasurer to warn that money would soon run out but now he had to explain that there was no money for them to continue their labors on the building.

I returned after a most blessed experience in southeast Asia to a full-blown acrimonious division upon the campus. I had traveled long, arriving home at four o'clock on a Tuesday morning. I had worked all day and after the prayer meeting I called a staff meeting to share God's great blessings upon our ministry in Southeast Asia. To my shock, for the first time in my Hartland experience, it took but a few minutes to realize that there was no joy in what God had accomplished. Many of the staff looked solemn, if not angry. I was puzzled by the staff's lack of enthusiasm for God's blessings. It was an atmosphere foreign to anything I had experienced before at Hartland. I soon realized, however, that there was no point in continuing to share God's leading and providences. Thus I stopped to ask the staff members to explain that which was troubling their minds. When the vocal members spoke out, their main concern was "We are in great debt; you should have been here to help solve the situation." I will never forget the positive reaction of Frances Lundberg. She was a new staff member then and she was thrilled to hear the report but she was certainly an exception in the situation. We were in a desperate crisis.

Recognizing the physician whom I had deduced as one of the leaders in the difficulties and who at this meeting had expressed great anxiety concerning the financial state of the institution, I asked him to walk with me after the meeting. He said that we were two hundred and seven thousand dollars in debt. I knew before we left for the Far East that we were in a serious financial operating situation, but I had not been informed it was at that level of magnitude. When we left, the debt was about seventy thousand dollars less than that. At that time in our development we were requiring about seventy thousand dollars to operate each month. I knew this increase did not happen in one month, because there would have been significant funds which would have flowed into the institution during the month. However, I wondered if our business manager had discovered invoices which had not been paid which had added to the deficit. By the time I finished discussing with the doctor it was too late to get in touch with the business manager. I spent a night of turmoil, determined that as soon as chapel was completed the next morning I would counsel with the business manager.

As soon as possible we were walking together and I quickly asked him, "What is our financial operating position?" He responded, "We are around one hundred forty thousand dollars in operating debt." Strangely I felt relieved, even though this was a very grave financial situation. We then reviewed all the fund balances and discovered that much was current debt (less than thirty days old), and quite a bit more had been placed in special funds which actually belonged in the general operating fund. Overall our real operating debt was about eighty-five thousand dollars.

I immediately called a meeting of the staff for that night, believing that it would be a great relief to all staff members and would solve the situation. Whenever misunderstandings had erupted at Hartland before, open dialogue speedily achieved resolution. But not this time! As soon as I had settled the financial issue, which was never seriously raised again, that segment of the staff who were hostile to our working relationships with Hope, and concerned about Hartland's relationship with the denomination, demanded to discuss what they believed was the wrong direction we were charting in cooperation with Hope International.

Let it be understood that there was never an organizational relation-ship with Hope International. As with other faithful workers for God we were, however, bonded together by cords of Christian love and a com-mon goal to spread the gospel message.

Prior to our leaving for the Far East, the whole issue had been heavily agitated by the Bible teacher. I feared this might continue while we were absent. I had penned a short note, and posted it to this Bible teacher from San Francisco airport, asking that he not agitate the situation while we were on the missionary trip and assuring him that we would do everything to address the issues upon my return. Clearly, however, he continued his agitation during my absence. By the time I returned almost half the staff was siding with him. Indeed, when a little later I took a secret ballot of the thirty-seven staff present, eighteen supported this Bible teacher's position and nineteen were favoring the determination to do everything that we could to be supportive of denominational entities, while remaining unwilling to compromise the goal of Hartland to work with all truth-loving individuals and ministries.

In spite of my plea that these issues not be aired with the students, this Bible teacher made his classes a forum to present his perspective. Not only was this to foreshadow the loss of what ultimately was at least a third of our staff, it also was the harbinger of the loss of a significant number of students—many of whom, I fear, were damaged for eternity by the confusion and uncertainty over what to believe. We had reached a point of impasse and I decided that the Bible teacher would have to leave. However, before I spoke with him, to my relief, he tendered his resignation.

I was passing through a mental torment such as I had never faced before in all my many years of administration. Of the four institutions in which I have held administrative positions, never once have they reached the level of conflict which was apparent at this time at Hartland. Nothing troubled me more than the total about-face of the Board Chairman, who had been my closest friend as we served together at Weimar Institute in California. Scores of times we had walked together, dialogued together, as our hearts beat in unison upon the gospel message and on the goals and the objectives of true education.

The Board Chairman had been thrilled to become part of Hartland's board and even more honored to be chosen later as chairman of the Board. He informed me that this was the greatest privilege of his whole life and he could think of nothing which was more important to him. But after a visit to the Netherlands, his whole attitude changed. Further, he was greatly influenced by a close friend of his who at the time was the Chairman of our Constituency. This man had taken the most aggressive stance against the issue of Hartland accepting tithe for its ministry. He also called for Hartland to refrain from preaching where there was opposition or lack of approval by denominational leaders. Neither of these positions could be sustained by Inspiration. Indeed, they were directly contrary to plain statements of the Bible and the Spirit of Prophecy.

> Do ye not know that they which minister about holy things live of the things of the temple? And they which wait at the altar are partakers with the altar? Even so hath the Lord ordained that they which preach the gospel should live of the gospel. —1 Corinthians 9:13, 14

> But watch thou in all things, endure afflictions, do the work of an evangelist, make full proof of thy ministry. —2 Timothy 4:5

The reader will remember that one of the conditions of my acceptance of the leadership of the new institution was the guarantee that truth would be the highest order of all things which we would seek to accomplish at Hartland. For the first time this ideal was being seriously challenged by members of the board who were convinced that our first loyalty was to follow church leaders. While we have been, and desire to be loyal to church leaders within the boundaries of Inspiration, the elevation of man's authority above God's was totally opposed to the goals, philosophy and mission of Hartland. While we believe in cooperation with denominational leaders, that cooperation ends when it would require compromise with the plain statements of Holy Writ. I made the decision that I would rather, much rather, leave Hartland, though it was so dear to my heart, than to compromise one whit the principles of heaven by following the directives of man.

As is often the case these principles were quickly interpreted as opposition to the "church" and "church leadership." There were those who rushed to declare that we were on a pathway of separation from the Seventh-day Adventist Church. Nothing could have been further from the truth and our subsequent history has proven the falsity of such accusations. On the other hand the words of inspiration were plain.

> A "Thus saith the Lord" is not to be set aside for a "Thus saith the church" or a "Thus saith the state." —*Acts of the Apostles*, 68

Indeed, we recognize that Jesus Himself, our great Exemplar, had to face the same issue in His day. Some of those Board members who opposed the foundational principles of Hartland were not silent. They were energetic in spreading their false reports far and wide concerning the principles of Hartland in its relationship to church organization. In this they exerted maximum damage upon God's holy work at Hartland. These reports were received sympathetically by most church leaders and many of our major donors. However, there is a God in heaven who is above all and over all and this great test was necessary to bind the staff, through the trauma of this situation, so that the true principles of heaven could continue in the ministry which God had so miraculously raised up.

# 22    The Miracle

*Now when Job's three friends heard of all this evil that was come upon him, they came every one from his own place; Eliphaz the Temanite, and Bildad the Shuhite, and Zophar the Naamathite: for they had made an appointment together to come to mourn with him and to comfort him.*                    —Job 2:11

A significant number of staff members had resigned and left Hartland before the October 1988 board meeting convened, partly because of the split over our principles. Quite a few of these were in key positions and some had been part of the pioneer staff. In the meantime I had received a number of threatening letters from the chairman of Hartland's Constituency demanding that I change my position on the tithe issue, or he would do everything he could to remove me as president of Hartland. Hartland Institute had followed divine counsel in respect to tithe. We did not solicit tithe; however when the Holy Spirit moved upon individuals to place their tithe with Hartland we carefully used it for ministry according to divine counsel, as did many other self-supporting ministries. This was in harmony with counsel from Church leaders up until this time. (See chapter entitled "The Affiliations.")

These threats from the chairman of the Constituency placed me very much where prayer and trust in God were my constant consolation. Some of the letters which passed between the chairman of Hartland's membership and me were published in the *Issues* book of 1992. I wrote to the individual concerned questioning why these were made public without my consent but received no reply. In 1988 I had responded to him kindly, but each time he responded with highly accusatorial letters, as revealed in the *Issues* book. This is an open document published by the North American Division and thus the tone of the chairman of the Constituency is on open record.

I told the Lord that, if it was His will, I would rather be dismissed from the leadership of Hartland than to dishonor Him or to walk in a path contrary to His Word. I have learned throughout my life that whenever I have followed the Word of God, I have never grieved over the decision made, but when I have followed what is not based upon the Word of God, I have greatly regretted the consequences.

The 1988–89 school year commenced with a much smaller student body. The work of the Bible teacher had led a significant number of students to choose other colleges in which to complete their training. He had led them to believe that Hartland was now following a very danger-ous path in opposition to the leaders of the Seventh-day Adventist Church. To add to the difficulties we faced, there had been a very strong crusade to poison the thinking of our major donors. This effort proved very suc-cessful and most of those who were influenced by this active campaign to destroy God's mighty work at Hartland have never again supported Hartland. The institution now faced a lowered student enrollment, the loss of at least one-third of the staff and the loss of almost every large donor to the institution.

Is it any wonder that rumors quickly surfaced claiming that Hartland Institute would soon collapse? How could it succeed when some of its most prominent staff had left? How could it continue when its student enrollment dramatically declined? How could it be sustained when its major donors had withdrawn their support and were influencing others to follow their lead? The answer to each of these questions was to be found in the words, "Trust in God and do the right." This we determined to do, in God's tender grace.

So comprehensive were the rumors that several months later I met a fellow Australian who had been a department leader in the General Conference, a man who had been a very good friend to me. Early in our conversation he asked, "Colin, where are you now?" I responded, "I am still at Hartland." He answered, "But Hartland closed." I had to inform him, "No one has told me that." He was amazed to know that Hartland was still functioning and functioning effectively. It took several years before the rumors concerning Hartland's demise or its imminent closure were to fade away.

The critical test for Hartland came at the October board meeting of 1988. It was well understood that this was to be a most difficult meeting. There was great apprehension among the administration and the staff, who realized that it was almost certain that a majority of the board members were opposed to the position which Hartland administration was following. Hartland had not changed its position from its beginning, but under pressure from Conference officers quite a number of the Board members had decided that we should follow Conference directives. These Board members now claimed that these Conference directives were consistent with inspiration. No definitive evidence was tended to support such claims.

Had we followed such a faulted course Hartland would now have been a thing of the past, and its divinely-inspired work would have failed. As most Conference administrations have led further into the promotion of error and faulted forms of worship, Hartland would have been brought down with them.

The Board meeting opened with a devotional, followed by the rendering of reports from the president, the treasurer and the divisional leaders. At this time I was the lone administrator seated as a voting member of the Board, although all other administrators were present and could contribute to the dialogue without participating in the voting. Unbeknown to us a significant number of the staff and students were meeting in my office during the Board meeting. They were praying and urging the Lord to overrule. Immediately as the Board meeting was opened for general business, the chairman of Hartland's Constituency, the one who had written the accusing letters to me, placed the following motion on the floor:

Therefore, in order to show our support and commitment and to seek harmony with the Seventh-day Adventist Church we hereby agree:

1. Never to receive tithe, knowingly, except it be provided by the General Conference of Seventh-day Adventists or its companion Divisions, or Conferences, and further affirmatively to teach others the sacredness of tithe and the obligation to return it to the Seventh-day Adventist Church.

2. To refrain from allying with or supporting any independent or self-supporting ministry which does not hold a similar high commitment to the Seventh-day Adventist church or which engages in any public criticism of it.

3. When any possibility for conflict exists, to secure approval from all affected Conferences, Unions, or Divisions before taking a Hartland Bible Conference, or similar activity, into any area.

The motion was quickly seconded. The dialogue on this motion continued uninterrupted for over five hours. So intense was the situation that lunch was brought to the Board members while they continued the dialogue without break. Early in the discussion it became clear that twelve of the members of the board strongly favored the motion and seven opposed it. In the more than five hours of dialogue and speeches not one person altered his or her position from the first speech which he or she had made. All members spoke many times. I believe God held His hand over the situation because at any time "question" could have been called upon the motion and the motion voted. Somehow this did not occur.

I realized that all six administrators would resign and seek to reestablish an institution somewhere else if the motion was voted. However this was never expressed to the Board members. Much of the time my mind was contemplating the questions, "When can we have an institution which is willing to honor God fully and follow His Word implicitly?" "Where should we turn to relocate such an institution?" These questions filled my tortured mind.

Alpine Springs Academy in Wisconsin came to mind. I knew it was in considerable difficulty and perhaps would be open to takeover by another ministry. I also thought of Groveland Academy in Florida. This academy had operated well for many years, but as the founders aged, it was no longer truly functioning as an academy. All my thoughts were a sign of limited faith. I glanced at the clock. It was about four o'clock, almost five hours since we had begun the dialogue on the motion.

With great heaviness of heart I slipped out of the meeting while the dialogue continued. I entered the large cafeteria, where I was alone. On my knees I prayed one of the most earnest prayers of my life, "Dear Lord, we are through. There is nothing more we can do to save this institution from taking a U-turn in its direction. All we have is Your help, and if You still have a purpose for Hartland Institute, please work a miracle." With that simple prayer I returned to the meeting.

I was sitting to the right of the Board chairman and Brother Richard Mayer, the vice-chairman, was seated to the left of the chairman at the head of the oblong tables. I noticed an unused paper napkin in front of me. I took out my pen, trying to clear my beclouded mind so that I could write something to offer as an amendment.

In stumbling words I wrote to the effect that Hartland was faithful, and by God's grace would always remain faithful, to the Seventh-day Adventist church. The words seemed feeble and ineffective, but nevertheless I passed the napkin around the back of the Board chairman to Brother Richard Mayer, the vice-chairman. The dialogue continued about another ten minutes, after which time Brother Mayer raised his hand for the attention of the chairman. He was given the floor. "I move an amendment to the motion, Mr. Chairman," and then he read what I had passed to him some minutes before. I quickly seconded the proposed amendment. With a little uncertainty in his voice the Board chairman said, "An amendment to what?" Brother Mayer hesitated for a moment and I responded, "An amendment to the third clause of the motion." This was the clause which I could not support under any circumstances. It was the clause which said we would not preach unless we had the assurance of the support of denominational leaders. That was contrary to the gospel commission, and I knew that already we had been blocked from preaching by following such protocol in some places. I was convinced that, should we vote that motion, we could not be loyal to our Savior's commission.

I was not at all concerned about the second clause of the motion. While I understood that it was directed against Hope International, that ministry was not specifically named and I could confidently accept this clause because I too had no desire to be associated with truly dissident or divisive groups. Even the statement concerning the tithe was open to interpretation. While of course the formulator of the motion equated *church* with *denominational structure*, this definition of *church* is certainly false. Self-supporting work is undeniably an important segment of the Seventh-day Adventist church. The word *church* is used in many different ways in Inspiration, so there was some flexibility in it.

The miracle I had prayed for followed. With almost anticlimactic speed and little dialogue, the amendment was put to a vote, and it was passed by fourteen votes to four! There is a God in heaven who still today works miracles. What changed the minds of seven of the board members, only the God of heaven knows. Soon after, the motion as amended also passed by fourteen votes to four. God, in a most marvelous way, had saved His institution. Of course, the swirl of accusations and counter-accusations continued. Indeed they were to continue for many years and occasionally are still voiced, even though almost fifteen years have passed since that vote was taken. Yet the blessing of God is now available for all to see. As late as 2003 one sincere former student at Hartland College asked if I would explain to him how the Constituency had reinstated me as president after the Board had dismissed me. However, there had never been a motion by the Board to dismiss me as president, though it was possible that could have been in the minds of some Board members.

The Board chairman angrily accused me of manipulating the vote. I told him I was following my deep convictions. These ensuing fifteen years have plainly demonstrated the results of faithful loyalty to God, His Word and His church. With vibrant enthusiasm and purpose, Hartland

Institute has become a worldwide presence to uphold the strength of the Seventh-day Adventist faith, to lead many men and women to the kingdom of heaven, to train hundreds of precious young people in sacrificial service for God and man, and to help God's people to prepare for the kingdom of eternity. In 1988 Hartland Institute reached its nadir. God permitted us to be severely tested. In His gracious care for His work, Hartland's ministry increased significantly from that time on.

# 23  The Conflict

*Can two walk together, except they be agreed?* —Amos 3:3

ARTLAND'S regular Board meetings are held twice a year—in the spring and in the fall. The Constituency membership meetings are held once a year. In the early years the Constituency meetings were held toward the end of April. Later this date was changed to October in association with the October Board meeting and the fall convocation.

As word began to spread concerning the crisis which took place at the October Board meeting, deep concerns arose. On the one hand there was much apprehension concerning the viability of Hartland. Many questioned whether it could survive such a crisis. Many believed that Hartland would collapse financially. Such views were held by some of Hartland's most ardent supporters, for it was felt that without the support of some of the most generous donors the institution could not survive. While I had some misgivings, I was learning to exercise faith in God and I believed that some way God would raise the necessary funds for the needs of the institution. That He did in a mighty way.

However, there were other concerns. We faced the problem of continuing Hartland's programs with at least one-third of the staff leaving. Once again God brought some very fine people to fill the vacancies. Yet it was a difficult time. Some of the pioneers of Hartland were among those who left. Some were among the most prominent leaders in the institution. These men and women who had given their hearts and lives so sacrificially in the early days when the going was tough, departed at a time when they could have had the joy of seeing more fully God's blessings upon the institution, as have we who remained. From a human perspective, the future was very uncertain. While those who left may have made a serious mistake, a great debt of gratitude is owed by Hartland Institute for their pioneering efforts.

As Hartland approached the April 1989 membership meeting it was not difficult to sense rising tensions. It is, among their other responsibilities, the role of the members of the Constituency to choose the Board of Directors. Much would depend upon the response of the members to the events of the October Board meeting as to the ultimate future of Hartland. There was still the possibility that the membership would mandate a major change in the direction of Hartland, which some of the Board members were determined to enact. However, I felt a strange peace. I knew, perhaps more than anyone else, the magnitude of the miracle that God had worked at the Board meeting. My faith and trust was strong that God, who had worked that miracle, was not about to desert Hartland at the membership meeting. And indeed that proved to be the case.

It was amazing to see the numbers of Constituency members who attended that meeting. It certainly was the highest attendance up to that date. This led many to speculate that I had rallied people whom I knew were supportive of my position to come to the membership meeting. It is true that I had been encouraged so to do by a number of earnest supporters of Hartland, but my answer was uniform, "The God who brought us through the Board meeting is the same God who will take us through the membership meeting." I believed that if I depended upon the arm of flesh, I would lose the mighty arm of the Lord. Accusations swirled around for several years following that membership meeting, that I had added many to the membership and had manipulated the attendees. Nothing could be further from the truth. Indeed, I was able to stand before God and say that there was only one person whom I had encouraged to attend that membership meeting and that was my own wife, for as I said to her, "The future ministry which we will fulfill is dependent upon the outcome of this membership meeting. You need to be there to witness how God will work."

The membership chairman was unable to be present; heavy work responsibilities kept him from the meeting. Thus when the meeting opened the members voted Elder Dennis Priebe to occupy the chair. He filled that role with distinction at a time of greatest difficulty. Constantly he remained objective and calm when emotions flared. These outbursts arose from some who evidenced anger toward me and at the direction Hartland had followed. Others defending the true calling of Hartland were very sad to witness God's work being discussed in anger. I determined that I would say very little and that I would not vote on the major issues at the membership meeting, for I believed that it was God who would lead in the decisions that day.

My one major speech did not please some of my colleagues or some of the other members. I called for calmness and a Christlike spirit in spite of the obvious different perspectives pervading the minds of the Constituency members. Without prior dialogue with me, one of the staff members offered a motion that all Board members be asked to state where they stood on two of the three issues which had been raised at the board meeting in October. Once again there were those who believed that I had made the "bullets" for this staff member to fire. The truth was that it was his own decision and he had deliberately, as he told me later, not shared his intention with me, knowing that I would oppose it. I did oppose the motion because I believed that everyone has a right to his convictions and a right to speak out for those convictions. Otherwise what is the use of a board? It is important for Board members, as well as all staff, to have the right to speak their convictions. This must be received, however, in an environment of harmony upon the basic principles of the Institute philosophy of faithfully following divine injunctions. Hartland did not have this unity at that time. It is just as dangerous to appoint members to an institution board who do not believe its philosophy as it is to appoint staff who do not support all God's doctrines and standards. Harmony on key philosophy and doctrinal issues, founded upon the authority of the Word of God, is vital to the long-term success of any institution, whether denominational or self-supporting.

Overwhelmingly the motion to question all Board members was voted and every Board member present was asked what he believed concerning the matters that had been raised in October 1988. The two questions were: "Should Hartland preach where they have an invitation even if it is not supported by the local Conference organization?" and, "Should Hartland cooperate and associate with other institutions which believe the truth, but which may not be viewed favorably by the Conference?" As a result of these responses, eight of the twenty Board members were not reappointed to the Board. Though it was sad for me to see three of these Board members not retained, it was important that five of them be released. It was not because their perspective differed from the president or other staff. It was because those five members had greatly undermined the Institution among leaders of the church, and were primarily responsibility for the loss of confidence in Hartland by our major donors. A Board Member must forward the goals of an institution, be supportive of its direction, and respect its support base. It is the board member's responsibility to resign from the board if he or she cannot do that. Within that framework, board members have the right to express their views openly and freely, without fear of disfavor.

Eight new Board members were appointed at that time, some of whom, fourteen years later, are still members of the Hartland Board of Directors. In a mighty and unparalleled way God had saved Hartland.

There were some who judged that because Hartland had been blacklisted by denominational entities as a result of the false reports spread by unfaithful Board members, Hartland would no longer have the opportunity to continue effective ministry. How wrong, again, this prediction proved to be. The ministry of Hartland is far stronger and much wider in its influence than it has ever been in its history. It is measurably much stronger than it was in 1988–89 when this crisis climaxed. This has not been due to the outstanding administration, staff, Board members or Constituency members. It is the result of the decision of Board and staff members to follow the will of God! Everything that has come about for good is the result of His mighty miracle-working power.

# 24 The Decentralization

*And it came to pass on the morrow, that Moses sat to judge the people: and the people stood by Moses from the morning unto the evening. And when Moses' father in law saw all that he did to the people, he said, What is this thing that thou doest to the people? Why sittest thou thyself alone, and all the people stand by thee from morning unto even? And Moses said unto his father in law, Because the people come unto me to inquire of God: . . . And Moses' father in law said unto him, The thing that thou doest is not good. . . . Moreover thou shalt provide out of all the people able men, such as fear God, men of truth, hating covetousness; and place such over them, to be rulers of thousands, and rulers of hundreds, rulers of fifties, and rulers of tens.*

—Exodus 18:13-15, 17, 21

HARTLAND Institute today is one of the finest examples of the decentralized form of governance. While it has ever been my goal as president to be an effective delegator, nevertheless, there were certain facets of Hartland Institute which were highly centralized in its earlier years. This was especially true of its financial management. All the earned income was channeled to one central fund. Thus it was not possible to understand the financial health of the different divisions which comprise the Institution. This led sometimes to tensions between the administrators for, in these early days, it was very difficult to keep current with accounts payable. Thus the decision concerning which invoices should have payment priority was a most difficult one, made by the business manager. Sometimes those decisions were not well received by administrators who felt that they were responsible for generating strong revenue to support their division. They believed that the funds they needed and had received were consumed to supplement the payment of bills in weaker divisions. These leaders complained that their invoices were not being processed in a timely manner. Yet there was no effective way to determine if the claims were accurate. Some areas of Hartland's ministry languished for lack of funds, when they should have been more strongly supported..

Thus a subcommittee of the Board, the Organization and Finance Committee, led by Dr. Norman Peek, was appointed. This subcommittee also included Richard Mayer, Walter Langeneckert and Lester Ortiz. It was commissioned to develop a plan for decentralization. Brother Langeneckert, a staff member at Hartland at the time, had much financial experience both in Switzerland and Australia. The other three were members of the Board of Trustees of Hartland. The subcommittee worked over an extended period of time. They reviewed their report with me before it was rendered to the Board. On the whole they had done a very fine work. However, there was one section which I could not accept. They had recommended that I be given final veto power over decisions of the Administrative Committee. This was wholly contrary to my understanding of biblical leadership and the decentralized model we were seeking to achieve. Leaders are not to be controllers, dictators nor rulers; they are to be servants. The Holy Spirit is equally able to imbue all who serve God faithfully with wisdom. Our model is Christ, and in His words He explained the true principles of Christian leadership.

> But Jesus called them unto him, and said, Ye know that the princes of the Gentiles exercise dominion over them, and they that are great exercise authority upon them. But it shall not be so among you: but whosoever will be great among you, let him be your minister; and whosoever will be chief among you, let him be your servant: even as the Son of man came not to be ministered unto, but to minister, and to give his life a ransom for many.                    —Matthew 20:25–28

> Neither as being lords over God's heritage, but being ensamples to the flock. And when the chief Shepherd shall appear, ye shall receive a crown of glory that fadeth not away.                    —1 Peter 5:3, 4

That recommendation was removed from the final draft and a consultant was chosen to assist in the implementation of the plan. Eventually the decentralized model was voted by the Board of Hartland. Decentralization as a process began to be implemented almost immediately. However it took a number of years before full implementation and refinement could be achieved and a smooth flow of fiscal information developed.

There were those, especially in the business office, who were unhappy with the decentralized process. It required more work in the office for a period of time, since it was essential to develop the necessary system revisions to facilitate smooth function. One serious blunder was made. Under the strong urging of the consultant some of the departments and divisions elected to do most of their own accounting. This included the Wellness Center, Hartland Publications, Last Generation and Young Disciple. Only the finances of the College, Plant Services and World

Mission were processed fully by the business office. Unfavorable consequences followed.

1. An unacceptable amount of staff time was spent in accounting. Often the work was undertaken by inexperienced and under-trained staff. This choice created a number of challenges and threatened to undermine God's principle that fiscal matters be in the hands of well-trained and efficient staff.

2. Some who were less familiar with good accounting practices unwittingly employed very poor accounting procedures and made many mistakes.

3. The process proved very costly, especially for Hartland Publications, whose complicated accounting reached a point where it was compelled to employ a consultant for twelve months to unravel the accounting nightmare.

4. Because different divisions were employing different accounting software, the work load was increased. Hartland Publications was using different accounting software from the Wellness Center, and both had chosen different software from the Hartland Business Office, complicating data transfer.

5. It led to enormous paper work as every transaction passed back and forth between each division and the business office.

Many voices began to call for re-centralization. But the administration held to the decentralization goals and principles. It was realized that the problem was not the decentralization model, but lay in the poor implementation of the decentralization plan, mismatched accounting procedures, resistance to change by some staff and problems in changing human thinking patterns. All of these deficiencies made the first years of decentralization very difficult.

Eventually steps were taken to re-centralize the accounting processes in the business office, while still maintaining separate accounting for each division. We were thankful to have an excellent treasurer in Samuel Chin. Before he left Hartland, Business Manager Norman Allred had firmly insisted that all divisions and departments were to use the MAS-90 accounting software. Painstakingly Brother Chin worked through the implications until every division was working with one single accounting software package processed in the business office. The business office managed each division with its own separate and distinct accounting records and the paper work was reduced to a minimum as transactions were made electronically. Also, for the first time the administrators of each division, as well as the institution administration were able to determine the fiscal health of each division at any moment.

Once established upon sound procedures, the division leaders became responsible for the success and welfare of their divisions. This led to more considered and careful planning on their part.

How thankful we were to the Lord to have had such an experienced and careful treasurer to work through the dilemmas. Now we receive the most detailed monthly reports of any self-supporting institution of which I am aware. This involves the many restricted accounts which we hold, the operational accounts and the financial position of each division. We have a clear understanding of the income as well as the expenses and it provides for us the opportunity to rectify problems much earlier than we could under the old system. Now we can identify any looming serious fiscal issues early, identifying the division experiencing difficulties. Thus remedial measures can be taken early. Periodically Brother Chin continues to update and refine the accounting procedure. This has been much approved and acknowledged by our external auditor.

Another important aspect of decentralization was the limits set upon the Administrative Committee (Ad Com). Prior to decentralization the Ad Com was permitted to involve itself in some of the day-to-day decisions of each division. After decentralization the Ad Com had decision-making responsibility only for matters which affected the whole institution or involved the work of a number of divisions.

Every divisional administrator was given a high level of autonomy in the operation of his or her division or department and in the choice of staff. Only when decisions concern the whole institution or require the involvement of, or impact upon, other divisions do those issues come for resolution to the Administrative Committee. Otherwise divisional leaders make those decisions, often in consultation with their staff members. The intervention of the treasurer and/or the president takes place only when there is a significant fiscal or spiritual problem in the making of a decision. However, both of us stand ready to offer counsel and advice at any time wherever needed and whenever requested.

These changes greatly enhanced the unity of the administrators by providing them freedom to determine the destiny of their own divisions within the mission guidelines, goals and purposes of the Institute. It also has provided a strong procedure for preparing the annual budget by the treasurer, allowing for review and recommendations by Ad Com and final review and approval by the Board of Directors. Furthermore, it has relieved the administration of the difficulties of seeking financial solutions with inadequate information. If a financial problem arises, administration can now much more easily address the problem at an early stage.

While recognizing the outstanding work of our present Treasurer, Samuel Chin, I acknowledge the efforts of previous business leaders in what has been a most difficult time when funds were scarce. Brother Chin was preceded by Hal Mayer, Georgia Parmalee, Rich Moseanko, Bob Puelz, Adell McMacken, Leonard Willett, David Tripp and Norman Allred. The choice of staff is one of the most important elements of any institution. When Hartland receives an application, it is reviewed by all administrators to determine whether any division has an interest in the services of the applicant. If there is an interest, then a telephone interview follows and references are checked. If there is still an interest, then the applicant is brought to Hartland for an extensive interview. This interview allows the Administrative Committee members and the applicant to obtain more information on which to base the decision as to whether the Lord is leading that individual to be part of the Hartland team. As far as possible all administrators participate in the interview. The interview can be quite lengthy. First spiritual life and doctrinal beliefs of the applicant are addressed. Family size and the spiritual lives of spouse and children are also carefully evaluated.

Only after the administration has been satisfied with the applicant's spiritual and doctrinal compatibility with Hartland Institute, does the interview move to the skills relevant to the position for which the applicant has applied. There is always earnest prayer to decide whether or not an applicant should be appointed to the staff. The Administrative Committee may turn down an applicant only on three issues:

**1.** If the committee is not satisfied with the evidence of the spiritual life of the applicant,

**2.** If there are significant questions about the doctrinal compatibility of the applicant, including the God-given standards that are upheld by Hartland staff and students, or

**3.** Lack of sufficient finances in the division where it is proposed to assign the applicant. The division leader must justify every financial expenditure. The leader must demonstrate that the department has the finances to support the applicant. This matter is routinely determined before an applicant is invited to an interview.

Usually, if an applicant is being considered to replace a departing staff member the financial issue does not arise because each division has an annually approved number of staff positions. The exception occurs when the cost for supporting the new staff member is much higher than for the previous staff member. This could happen if the previous staff member is single and the new applicant is a married man with a wife who would not be working, and the family had a number of children. Such an applicant could more than double the cost to the division. This situation could lead to the Administrative Committee vetoing the application, if no other adjustments to offset the additional cost can be found, or if no additional revenue is available to meet the additional expense.

Once the three key areas have been cleared by the Administrative Committee, the divisional leader has full authority to accept the applicants whom he or she believes would best fit into the needs of the division. In following these practices there has been a significant elevation in the unity among the members of the Administrative Committee, and this has also increased the cooperation between divisions.

God certainly has been leading and guiding Hartland as we seek to come ever closer to His divine pattern. Hartland Institute strives to be a model to the students of how institutions which God raises up to His glory and to the hastening of His coming are best operated.

# 25 The New Ministries

*And he said unto them, Go ye into all the world, and preach the gospel to every creature.*                    —Mark 16:15

IT has ever been the desire of Hartland to see new ministries established—ministries which will be profitable for the Lord's work around the world. Interest is not limited to those raised up by Hartland's graduates, former staff or students; nevertheless it is gratifying to us to see ministries being raised up by Hartland's graduates and staff. These will increase as God's work goes forward. Though we would have been delighted to see these new ministries raised up earlier, yet there needed to be a strengthening and development of the home base at Hartland before this could be expected to take place. The principles which God has implemented at Hartland Institute are necessary to successful ministries and will be studied carefully by those who are raising up new self-supporting organizations. With the closure of Madison College, the pattern self-supporting institution, in 1964, Hartland Institute personnel take very seriously the responsibility of providing a model which God would approve for other such institutions to follow.

Today there are ministries established or being established in Australia, Sweden, Malaysia, Ecuador, Zimbabwe, Ghana, Great Britain, the United States, Honduras, Dominican Republic and India. All trace their beginnings to the impetus gained from Hartland Institute. One of the finest of these is led by Lyle Southwell: it is Higher Ground in Australia. This ministry, located near Sydney, is a revival, evangelistic and literature ministry which also trains lay evangelists. Scott Charlesworth and Mark Roberts, two former Hartland students, had leading roles in this ministry in its beginning days. Higher Ground continues to be a highly respected ministry around Australia and is certainly in good hands under the leadership of Lyle Southwell, who came to Hartland from the island state of Tasmania.

Lia Institute, in Sweden, had its foundations in Hartland. It was planned at Hartland College. Every second year I teach a class in Principles of Self-Supporting Work to the students of Hartland. One of the major responsibilities of the class is to present an extensive project for a proposed ministry. Any country in the world may be chosen. Any valid ministry can be the focus. The plans can be undertaken on an individual basis or as a group with up to four students working together. This has been a tremendous help to many students. A comprehensive plan has to be well developed in detail. The students are required to present a realistic, not a fanciful, project.

The Lia Institute in Sweden began as a project in the Principles of Self-Supporting Work class. It was led by Claus Nybo, a student from Denmark. He was able to interest a number of other students to join him in the project. So serious was this group that over a long period of time its members met with me once a week to discuss the development of their plans. They also met regularly with Brother and Sister Hal and Betsy Mayer and other staff. Lia was to be established as a training center for European students to help educate an army of youth in Europe to take the everlasting gospel to the world. Eventually a genuine plan began to develop. Brother Hal Mayer was asked to serve on its board, and great interest in Scandinavian and other European countries developed.

In spite of many problems and difficulties, Lia began to train a fine group of workers for the cause of Christ. Some are already working diligently in Europe, others have chosen to serve overseas in mission work.

Sadly however, events began to develop that eventually led to disaster. The difficulties reached such a magnitude that in 2002 Lia had to vacate its original premises in what can only be termed a hostile takeover by those who espouse separationism. Daniel Garcia, who has been its successful leader, is now seeking a new location in Portugal. It is hoped that the project will not be abandoned and that its best days will be in the future. God will not abandon Europe.

Peter Gregory, a 1992 graduate of Hartland College, has established Iona Research Center, a ministry designed to train Bible workers for God's cause. Peter, a Korean by birth, operates this short-term evangelistic training school with a small number of students each year. It is presently located in California.

David Fam, a Chinese-Malaysian, graduated from the Health Ministries major in 1995. He has now established a wellness center near Malacca, Malaysia. David has engendered strong support for this ministry, and it has helped many with their physical diseases and their spiritual needs. A number of Malaysian students have enrolled in Hartland College as a result of their earlier training in Brother Fam's wellness center, just as has been the case from Lia Institute.

Sebastian Teh (graduate of 1990), and his wife, Cynthia, have established a ministry for China. While it is impossible for them to locate their ministry *in* China, their efforts are for the benefit of China. They have done a fine work in sending literature into China, networking, preaching and in health ministry. Sebastian, an ethnic Chinese, is also a native of Malacca, Malaysia, while Cynthia is a native of Beijing, China. Wong Kok Boon, another ethnic Chinese and native from Malacca and a Health Ministries graduate of 1993, is now ministering in mainland China with his wife and family.

Ray De Carlo (graduate of 1989) has established his ministry in Maryland. Ray has an evangelistic and revival ministry and has brought many souls to Christ and into the Seventh-day Adventist faith. He has also held very successful lay evangelism schools while serving in many countries of the world.

In Zimbabwe, Trustmore Parangeta (graduate of 2000) has established a soul-winning ministry centered in Harare, the capital of Zimbabwe. He, too, has been rewarded with souls for the kingdom in that troubled country.

On a larger scale, Josephine Moyo, a Health Ministries graduate of 2000, a native Zimbabwean, has established a training school in Redcliff, Zimbabwe.

In Ecuador, the Salazar family is in the process of establishing an educational center not far from the capital, Quito. All three children have graduated from Hartland Institute—Esteban, 1999; David, 2000; and Stephanie, 2002. All are contributing to the establishment of this Institution.

Hartland World Mission, under the direction of Frances Lundberg, has been responsible for opening self-supporting institutions in Ghana and Nigeria. Former staff members, Brother and Sister Joe Willis have a strong health ministry in Honduras with several clinics for the care of the mountain people.

Another former staff couple, Pastor Maurice Berry (pastoral evangelism graduate 2002) and his wife have established a ministry in southern Virginia for evangelistic training. Brother and Sister Ron Goss, former staff members, are operating an outreach and evangelistic ministry, Project Resore, also in Virginia. John and Dorothy Davis have established a publishing ministry in northern California. The Evert family are publishing the excellent *Young Disciple* magazine which was first developed by Sister Evert at Hartland. They are now operating this ministry from Washington state. It is an excellent alternative to the compromised junior and teenaged level denominational publications for this age group. Charley and Dolly Tompkins in California now publish the Ellen G. White *Sabbath School Lesson Comments* which also had its beginnings at Hartland Institute.

A brother-sister team, Male Bone, Pastoral Evangelism class of 2003, and Nella Laing, Christian Elementary Education class of 2001, are establishing another ministry in East Malaysia in the state of Sabah, their home state. Male Bone has also taught and evangelized on almost all continents. Robert Pannekoek (Health Ministries in 1996 and Pastoral Evangelism in 1997), from Australia, has chosen to have a traveling ministry which has led him to preach and evangelize on most of the continents of the world. Robert is a fully qualified health educator as well as an evangelist.

Other graduates such as Adam Ramdin of England and Glenn Peters, a native of Trinidad, both of whom graduated in 2001 from the Pastoral Evangelism major, are also traveling evangelists. Sheri Trueblood from Massachusetts (Bible Instructor graduate, 1999) is a most successful soul winner in the United States and overseas. These are but some of the former students and staff of Hartland who are distinguishing themselves in ministry for the Lord.

Other institutions which have their foundation in the ministry of Hartland Institute include the Gazeley Bible Fellowship which was established in 1986 following a Hartland Bible Conference which was held in the old rectory in the village of Gazeley in Suffolk, England. It brings great encouragement to see what is now a rapidly growing list of ministries around the world. However, there are many more institutions which Hartland has assisted—institutions which are greatly appreciated and which have demonstrated their loyalty to the task of hastening the coming of our Lord.

Many Hartland graduates and former students have chosen to work in some of the already existing self-supporting institutions. Many are teaching and ministering in academies operated by lay ministries. Some of these include Chester Clark, Shawnta Moore, David Preisner, Steven Conway, Linda Shin, Nigel Standish and Michelle Patterson. Others have developed individual ministries.

Some graduates have chosen to minister in the organized work. The only reward to Hartland College is in seeing its graduates and former students firmly planted on the platform of truth and righteousness and ministering to hasten the coming of our Lord Jesus Christ.

Hartland College also acknowledges the fine contribution that some of its graduates have made to their alma mater. They have included outstanding Bible teachers, health workers, educators and publication workers. Bible teachers have included Ray DeCarlo, Peter Gregory, Emanuel Baek, Robert Pannekoek, Maurice Berry and David Shin. Health ministry workers have included Alena Wehr (née Johnson), Electra Covington (née Davis) and Maria Gligor. Educators have included Chuck Holtry and Amy Lawaty. Still others have served in publishing work. These include Rose Rogers (née Heinrich); Michael Prewitt; Daniel Pedley and his wife, Antonella (née Assimiti); Ted Evert and his wife, Christina (née Boyd); Tony Evert and his wife, Sylvia (née Williams).

In November–December Remnant Herald camp meetings in Australia in the year 2002, I was delighted to meet with former Hartland students. At the Melbourne camp I met with six, at the Sydney camp (held by Remnant Herald in conjunction with Higher Ground Ministry) I met with four, and at the Brisbane camp (held in conjunction with ALMA Ministry) with four. On all continents I meet former Hartland students working faithfully in the cause of God. It brings me profound satisfaction and great joy.

I was shocked recently when Sheri Trueblood said to me, "Hartland graduates are like the Jesuits." I responded that I hoped that was not true. Then she relieved my mind by adding, "They are ministering all over the world." That army of youthful workers is earnestly seeking to save the lost. There can be no doubt that this growing army equipped with the two-edged sword of the Spirit, the Word of God, is destined to play a mighty role in the spread of the three angels' messages worldwide.

# 26 The Graduates

*These schools [of the prophets] were intended to serve as a barrier against the wide-spreading corruption, to provide for the mental and spiritual welfare of the youth, and to promote the prosperity of the nation by furnishing it with men qualified to act in the fear of God as leaders and counselors.* —Education, 46

THE most commonly heard question concerning Hartland graduates is, "What do they do when they graduate from Hartland College?" The answer is, "Most of them work earnestly for the Lord." Of course, that is a general answer. The answer is more specific when we address the majors. First let me address the graduates from the pastoral-evangelism and Bible instructors majors. Most of these graduates choose some form of self-supporting ministry. The ministries have varied widely. Some have been chosen to evangelism as roving preachers around the world. Others have established ministries and from these operate their evangelism. Quite a few have followed a calling into mission service while others are leaders in the literature work. Some are college and academy Bible teachers, academy deans and chaplains. A few have established, or helped to establish, their own self-supporting school. Some have become evangelists and Bible workers in the media field including *Amazing Facts* and *It is Written*. At least two are self-supporting academy administrators.

Those who have joined denominational work are pastoring, usually with an emphasis upon soul-winning evangelism. Quite a few are in youth ministry and fulfill almost all the roles enunciated above in self-supporting work. One is a Conference evangelist and another has been a departmental leader in a foreign Mission. As of the preparing of this book, ten of Hartland's graduates are ordained ministers. Already thousands of souls have been led by Hartland's graduates to the Lord and many of these converts themselves are now effective and enthusiastic workers for the Lord.

Health ministries graduates are also blessed with varied options. Some are serving in health and wellness centers while others have ministered in connection with physicians as health care practitioners and nutritional and exercise physiology consultants. A few have become community health counselors. Others have established their own health and ministry institutions. Such institutions have become established by graduates in Malacca, Malaysia and Redcliff, Zimbabwe; Ecuador; Sydney, Australia. Others have served in Dominican Republic, Honduras, Mexico and Sweden.

Christian elementary and secondary education graduates are in great demand both for self-supporting and denominational institutions. We cannot supply graduates for all the calls we receive. A number are now principals both of self-supporting and denominational schools. Others are serving in administrative rolls. While most are teaching in elementary or secondary schools, others teach at the college level. Several have served as academy deans.

The newest major, Christian Publication Management, while yet graduating relatively small classes, has generated a great demand for our graduates. Some have served in self-supporting institutions. Some have accepted calls to self-supporting ministries such as Outpost Centers Incorporated and 3ABN Television. One is serving in the North American Division Communications Department of the General Conference. A number of others are serving overseas.

Many anxious parents wonder what opportunities are available for graduates from an unaccredited college. There are over one hundred and sixty unaccredited colleges and universities in California alone. Many well-established institutions for various advantages choose not to seek regional accreditation. This choice in no way leads to the automatic conclusion that they are academically weak and inferior. Indeed some are renowned for their educational excellence. Hartland has chosen to remain unaccredited so that we can achieve a program of highest excellence in order to train our students to be the most intelligent workers for God. It is evident that our accredited colleges have failed disastrously to educate gospel workers trained to be powerful witnesses to proclaim God's end-time messages. Many are unable to present the everlasting gospel of the three angels, the Sanctuary message, the message of Christ Our Righteousness and such truths central to salvation.

Hartland graduates stand out because they have been immersed in the Bible and Spirit of Prophecy—not in the theology of men. It is easy to identify a Hartland preacher. My wife and I visited the Burnt Mills Church in the Potomac Conference one Sabbath. Unbeknown to us it was "Youth Emphasis Sabbath." We did not know that the speaker for the divine service was to be a former Hartland student. He preached a very challenging service which reached the hearts of the youth. Visiting that day was a family from upstate New York. After the service they approached me explaining that part way through the service the wife nudged her husband, whispering, "This speaker must have come from Hartland College. You don't hear speakers like this from other colleges."

Similar identifications were made at churches in Adelaide and Sydney, Australia. These young men have been trained to preach present truth. They stand out from the general graduates from denominational colleges. They possess preaching skills that are becoming rarer today. Hartland graduates possess a profound understanding of God's Word. They excel academically. Most of all, their characters testify to their love of Jesus. Whenever they preach to young people the souls of the youth are drawn to the matchless claims of Christ. There is an absence of contemporary music, drama or entertainment, but the hearts of the youth recognize that they are hearing the message for which they are hungering.

The Health Ministry majors are trained, not only to restore the physical health of the body, but to lead souls to the kingdom of eternity. Our graduates have seen the gospel message transform the lives of men and women broken in both body and soul. Likewise education and publishing graduates have also focused upon preaching, evangelism and soul winning. We have some fine visible workers spreading out around the world. They believe that the healthiest state of all is eternal life. Thus they earnestly seek the salvation of those whose physical needs they serve.

While it is not the result of counsel from the college, some of our graduates have very successfully undertaken graduate work—some at the top of their classes.

Having been the president of two denominationally-operated colleges, it has been my experience that we had more difficulty in placing these graduates than our graduates from Hartland. God brings young men and women to Hartland to train for His service and provides the perfect place for them to serve.

Presently we are seriously dialoguing the role of our graduates in the future of Hartland Institute. Conventional worldly academic wisdom is that staff should be chosen from a wide diversity of academic institutions so as to provide a broad spectrum of ideas and experience. This philosophy certainly serves the goals of secular institutions, but we believe the need to be quite different for a specially-raised-up, God-centered institution. We believe our graduates are the best pool of potential workers for their alma mater. They know intimately the goals, practices, and destiny of the institution. Already quite a number of graduates have served with distinction at their alma mater.

Our graduates are the testimony to the power of the gospel and the divine calling of Hartland Institute. They are not just another graduate. They are young men and women who have a thorough knowledge of the everlasting gospel and of the pillars of our faith. They minister with the grace and power of the gospel. They are honoring God, the church and their alma mater. They are forming an army to take the gospel to the world. Simply stated, they love their Savior with their entire hearts. Their greatest joy is humbly to serve Him.

Thus we are researching all our graduates so that we can provide an up-to-date profile of their post-college experiences, their level of performance, their loyalty to truth and righteousness. We are asking our graduates to be ready, wherever possible, if ever needed, to fill a vacancy at their alma mater. It is our plan, under the Holy Spirit's guidance, to do all to secure the goals of a pattern institution. We will be looking for graduates to fill the role of Board members when vacancies occur. We will also review the suitability of graduates to fill vacancies in the staff in the various divisions. Further we will seek those graduates with high aptitude to be trained to take over senior administrative positions including divisional leadership. We believe that within our graduate pool are many who will have the integrity to uphold the foundational objectives of Hartland and to move the institution forward to the completion of its mission when the time has arrived that the gospel will be shared with every inhabitant of the planet. Of course this will in nowise mean that we will not consider the appointment of other faithful Seventh-day Adventists to positions of trust. It is my earnest goal that Hartland will figure prominently with all other faithful saints in the final work on earth.

# 27    The Future

*And the people served the L*ORD *all the days of Joshua, and all the days of the elders that outlived Joshua, who had seen all the great works of the L*ORD, *that he did for Israel.*    —Judges 2:7

WHAT the future holds for Hartland Institute, only the infinite mind of God knows. Yet the past can be remembered and its lessons learned. Sister White has indicated that schools of a different order will be established at the end of earth's history (*Counsels to Parents, Teachers, and Students*, p. 532). These schools are not established after the schools of the world, nor after the schools which we have established in our past history, but after the pattern of the Eden school, after the pattern of the school of Christ. Hartland College is one of those schools. Clearly Hartland is not patterned after the schools of the world. But there are a number of reasons why it is not patterned after the Seventh-day Adventist schools established in the past.

The first Seventh-day Adventist colleges had a rocky beginning. That first college, Battle Creek College, was established in 1874 on seven acres (soon after to be reduced to five acres) and was located in the city. Sister White said she wept: Professor Sidney Brownsberger, the first president frankly admitted that he knew not how to develop a college according to the principles outlined by the servant of the Lord. He thus established a college that required five years' study of classical Greek and Latin. There were no required Bible classes, though Uriah Smith did teach an optional Bible class. Meat was routinely served in the cafeteria. There were later reforms, but more than twenty years elapsed before a college was thoroughly established on proper principles, and that was in Australia.

Two schools were established as pattern schools—Avondale College, first called the Avondale School for Christian Workers, established in Australia in 1897, and Madison College, Tennessee, established 1904. Sister White superintended the development of Avondale College and it was she who designated it the pattern school. Some have called it the blueprint school. It was established to be the model which would serve as the example for all future Seventh-day Adventist colleges. I have therefore studied very closely the early years of Avondale College. It has special significance to me as I graduated from it (1951) and was chairman of Avondale College's Education Department for five years from 1965–1969 inclusive.

The Madison school in Tennessee in the United States was established as a self-supporting college in 1904 to be a model for other self-supporting colleges. The founding leaders of Hartland carefully studied the history of this school also. In a profound way, Hartland reflects these model institutions. However today, neither can be looked to as a contemporary model. Madison College closed its doors for the last time in 1964 after sixty years of training young people. I have studied very carefully the reasons for the ultimate demise of that institution. In brief I record some of my observations concerning the factors contributing to its failure.

**A.** Madison had a powerful foundational leader, but never was there a subsequent leader who could compare with Dr. E. A. Sutherland in leadership ability. This is always a great danger, for very few institutions, either self-supporting or denominational, improve in godliness after the departure of their first leader. Those which do rarely survive well after their second leader. Either the departure of the second leader leads to closure or the third president leads the institution in another direction, away from the perfect plan and pattern of Christ. This history is a repetition of Old Testament times—Moses, Joshua, Elijah, Elisha. Thus Hartland Institute Board has an urgent responsibility to find an outstanding younger man to train to serve as the next president of Hartland Institute. He needs to be a man who—

1. Is totally dedicated to God;

2. Would rather die than commit one wrong word or action;

3. Has a deep understanding of God's Word and is committed to all the true principles of Christian education;

4. Will not waver from God's truth, and will not be swayed by plausible or intriguing winds of doctrine;

5. Is humble and sincere;

6. Has considered and wise judgment;

7. Understands both the theory and practice of the Christian life;

8. Is an effective teacher and preacher of the Word;

**9.** Is of the highest moral rectitude and honesty;

**10.** Has a stable temperament and is of calm but firm resolution;

**11.** Understands the true qualities of the servant-leader and will eschew all centralized or autocratic forms of governance;

**12.** Will make important decisions only after searching for the will of God in Holy Scripture and inspired writings and counseling widely with godly colleagues;

**13.** Is willing to sacrifice;

**14.** Will safeguard the sacred hours including the edges of the Sabbath, and has courage and fortitude;

**15.** Will ensure that each staff member has proven by test and trial that he loves God and works in the ways of righteousness;

**16.** Will develop the programs of the college to reflect the fullness of true physical, intellectual and spiritual balance in the program of both students and staff;

**17.** Is loving and compassionate, especially to the fallen;

**18.** Has skill in careful fiscal management;

**19.** Has chosen a godly wife compatible with the above goals, and has—or will—train his children in the ways of righteousness;

**20.** Engenders confidence from the Constituency, Board, administration and staff.

I am convinced that the most suitable candidate for leadership will be an experienced educator who is also a powerful presenter of God's present truth.

You may say it is impossible to find all these characteristics in one individual. This may be true. But if he has most of these qualities, he will pray to God for the wisdom of Solomon, asking for God to enhance his talents where he is deficient. He will seek to gather about him a dedicated, consecrated, talented staff to employ his strengths and complement his weaknesses so that at least all these characteristics are to be found in the administrative team. Above all, such a leader needs to surrender to Christ every day, listening to His voice and following in all His ways. Such a leader will direct Hartland Institute to higher ground and to prepare a people to receive the latter rain, to finish the gospel commission and herald the coming of our blessed Lord and Savior.

**B.** The second lesson to be learned from the failure of Madison is to stand unwaveringly against accreditation. It must have been an anguished Dr. Sutherland who eventually yielded to a controlling influence he knew was inimical to the principles of heaven. He allowed a human organization to intervene between the words of God and himself. One can understand the reasons for which Sutherland took this step, but we can never condone that faulted decision. Sutherland was a great Christian educator, maybe the greatest this church has known, but the consequences of his wrong decision were tragic.

Many years into the Madison experience, Dr. Sutherland received a communication from his cofounder, Dr. Percy Magan, then the Administrator of the College of Medical Evangelists (now Loma Linda University). Dr. Magan informed Sutherland that unfortunately the College of Medical Evangelists could no longer continue to accept the graduates of Madison College into the medical program unless Madison College was accredited. It had been believed for many years that graduates from Madison College were given preference over graduates from Seventh-day Adventist denominational colleges in the selection of entrance into Loma Linda Medical School. This had brought great prestige to Madison and the number of its students increased until it reached about five hundred. This size was comparable to that of many of the denominational colleges at that time. No doubt Dr. Sutherland reasoned that, should Madison graduates no longer be accepted at Loma Linda, there would be a rapid decline in applicants to attend Madison College, and this assumption may have been correct. But we must ever trust God, and do the right.

The pressure was great but the consequences of accreditation were fatal to the survival of the institution, and were to serve the purposes of Satan which led to the demise of this model institution. Madison's enrollment would no doubt have decreased unless God had specifically intervened. In any case, Madison was already nearly twice the size recommended by Sister White. She had declared that Battle Creek College was too large and had attracted too many families to locate near the college for the education of their children. She said that funds expended at Battle Creek should have been used to establish other smaller institutions. At the time, Battle Creek College had about one thousand students, three times as large as inspiration suggested.

If two-thirds of the people in Battle Creek were plants of the Lord in other localities, they would have room to grow. Greater results would have appeared if a portion of the time and energy bestowed on the large school in Battle Creek to keep it in a healthy condition had been used for schools in other localities where there is room for agricultural pursuits to be carried on as a part of the education. Had there been a willingness to follow the Lord's ways and His plans, many plants would now be growing in other places.        —*Testimonies*, Vol. 6, 211, 212

Maybe Dr. Sutherland thought of the staff who would have to be released, or the lack of prestige that would ensue in such circumstances. This is a warning not to increase the size of Hartland beyond that which will permit the effective training of young people to be leaders at the end of time in the proclamation of the gospel to every nation, kindred, tongue and people.

C  As Madison's sanitarium became popular and financially prosperous, it was decided to raise significantly the salaries of the staff. Some of the sanitarium staff argued that it was unfair to keep salaries so low. While the salaries of the sanitarium staff were raised significantly, there was no commensurate rise in the salaries of the college staff. This decision was disastrous. A rise in the salaries *per se* would not have had nearly the impact, had it been spread over the whole of the institution, including the college staff. However, once the differential was made between the two divisions of Madison Institute, dissatisfaction arose among the college staff, challenging the harmony of the institution. When the accreditation team from the Southern Association of Schools and Colleges arrived for the scheduled accreditation visit and evaluation, some of the college staff were not slow to express their dissatisfaction with the salary base which they were receiving.

Of course, the secular evaluation team noted this as a grave weakness. They were concerned not so much with the fact that the salaries were low, but that there was a significant difference between the salaries of those with much the same responsibilities in the college when compared with those of the sanitarium. They noted that workers in the administration and in the business side of both divisions of Madison had significantly different remuneration scales. Those who were teaching in the health department, or anywhere there was a similarity of responsibility, would naturally be attracted to the sanitarium by its salary scale rather than to the college, if provided the choice. The accreditation team argued that it was now not possible for the college to attract the best staff because the better staff would choose to serve in the sanitarium where the salaries were considerably higher. Therefore the accreditation team mandated greatly increased salary remuneration for the college staff. Valiantly the college attempted to sustain the new salary level. Some assistance was provided by the sanitarium, but not nearly enough. Little time passed before the college was in a perilous financial situation. This led Madison College to be gifted to the Southern Union in 1963. One year later the Southern Union closed the doors of the college forever. The Southern Union understandably argued that Southern Missionary College already served the needs of the Union and a second college was not needed.

The lessons Hartland must learn from Madison College include:

1.  Never accept any form of regional accreditation or governmental approval or outside control;

2.  Never permit the college to grow too large—certainly not beyond three hundred students; and

3.  Under no circumstances should there be any difference in the salaries for the various divisions of Hartland Institute, no matter the degree or lack of prosperity of any division. Should one division become very prosperous, its responsibility should be to help maintain the salaries of a weaker division. To fail in this respect will bring predictable conflict to the institution and the result ultimate catastrophe. It is axiomatic that every division cannot be equally profitable. It must be the selfless joy of the prosperous division leaders to aid divisions which are less favored.

4.  Do not gift a self-supporting institution to a Conference entity.

What lessons can be learned from Avondale College, the model denominational school? Avondale College is still functioning, over one hundred years after its establishment in 1897. But even the most ardent supporter of Avondale College would acknowledge that it has changed dramatically, having departed from the mission, goals, aims and objectives for which it was established under the guidance of God through the servant of the Lord.

Avondale College is my alma mater. With my twin brother Russell, I graduated in 1951 from the Theological Normal Course, translated into today's language, the Christian Teacher Training Course. Avondale College had been established to uphold the highest principles of Christian education, of moral integrity and of training in biblical principles. For half of the college's existence men and women were chosen as teachers not because of their academic degrees, but because of the quality of their knowledge of God's truth and the principles of God-centered teaching. Some members of the teaching staff did fail in these areas, but the objectives quoted above were held for some years.

About halfway through the twentieth century the emphasis upon academic degrees and staff professional training changed the focus. Men and women were often chosen to teach students at Avondale, not so much because of their integrity to the Seventh-day Adventist message and their knowledge of God's truth, but so that they might regale the institution with their degrees and academic brilliance.

By the time I was called to the Education Department of Avondale College in January 1965, that certainly was the case. I am convinced that the most attractive aspect of my appointment, as far as the college administration was concerned, was the fact that I had just successfully completed my Doctorate of Philosophy at the University of Sydney. I had the privilege of serving for five years as chairman of the Education Department. But the heartbreaking spiritual paralysis, the doctrinal deviation and the worldliness that now pervade this institution are phenomenal. Academics and theological recognition have become far more important than doctrinal integrity and spiritual development.

A copy of a document prepared May 2002 by the Christian Research Association, entitled "Pastoral Research Survey, Seventh-day Adventist Minister Survey," is very revealing. This survey researched the attitudes and evaluations of Avondale College by pastors graduated there in the previous ten years. Without summarizing a sixty-four-page report which reveals heart-wrenching facts concerning the course content, training and internships of these graduates, it is clear that no longer are the ministers and, by extension, the other graduates being trained to present the three angels' messages to the world, to hasten the coming of Jesus and to prepare a people for the latter rain so that this final end-time message will be carried to every nation, kindred, tongue and people.

While the findings are no surprise to those who have been observers of the rapid decline in the mission and ministry of Avondale College, we draw a number of conclusions. Of course, Avondale College is only one example. A reference to any of the major denominational colleges in the

United States, and most of those in other parts of the world, would lead to very similar conclusions. Denominational colleges have departed from their foundational principles. Satan has found a way to refocus these institutions so that they have a form of godliness but deny the power thereof. Satan's nefarious goal is to destroy the education which is so necessary to train God's faithful workers. The servant of the Lord wrote,

> With such an army of workers as our youth, rightly trained, might furnish, how soon the message of a crucified, risen, and soon-coming Saviour might be carried to the whole world!     —Education, 271

Of course, there must be well-trained, intelligent and capable teachers in our institutions. But first and foremost they must be thoroughly Seventh-day Adventist; they must pass the test of unwavering belief in the Seventh-day Adventist pillars and demonstrate spiritual commitment and moral integrity. All constituency members, board members, administrators and staff members must be dedicated Seventh-day Adventists. No staff members are presently serving at Hartland unless they have passed a very extensive interview in which their beliefs, their spiritual life and their characters have been assessed in personal interviews. Only after those tests have been passed are staff applicants then evaluated for other aspects of their preparation for the ministry to which they are called.

Vigilance in these matters must always be maintained. Godly, knowledgeable, well-informed, earnest Christians practicing the morality of the Bible must be chosen, no matter what position they are called to fulfill. As God's people traverse the final days of this earth's history, it is increasingly important to uphold the highest standards for the Institute's staff and ministry. Academic qualifications are secondary to spiritual and godly commitment. Hartland seeks for staff who are thoroughly schooled in the Word of God. Worldly scholars and worldly theologians have no place at Hartland. Needed are men and women of godly integrity who evidence a deep knowledge and practice of God's Word. Every member of the staff must constantly keep these principles in mind.

When Hartland commenced, I stated, "If Hartland Institute is still functioning fifty years from now, there is a great likelihood that it already will be on the pathway to apostasy and worldliness." Almost certainly I would not be around then. Twenty years have passed, two-fifths of that fifty years are now history. I am now approaching my seventieth birthday. My love for God and for His Son Jesus Christ, my desire to live with Jesus throughout eternity, my love for souls, my special concern and love for our boys and girls and youth, has been the focus of my adult life.

I have dedicated my ministry with the hope that I can play a significant role in preparing the final generation to take this blessed message to
every nook and cranny of this world. The older I become, the more
earnest are my endeavors to this end. I am full of hope that in this
perverse world and in this compromised church there are still young men
and women who are overcoming "by the blood of the Lamb and by the
word of their testimony" and I believe that they love "not their lives unto
the death" (Revelation 12:11). While ever I have strength and energy,
while ever my mind is clear, my life is dedicated to training. I pray daily to
God that He will grant me health and strength, as long as He deems that I
can be fruitful to Him in this ministry. Yet it is inevitable in this world that
I will decline in strength. Therefore I must challenge every new staff
member never to deviate from the purpose for which the Institution was
established by the Lord:

1. Please read this book carefully as you take up your new responsibility. It will help you to understand the purposes, the struggles, the
vision and the passion of those who established this institution. By
God's grace it will help you to strengthen your commitment and
determination to permit not one minor compromise in the purposes
for which God established this institution.

2. I challenge all new staff members not to be satisfied with the
status quo, but to seek ways by which this institute will increasingly
model the paradigm God has provided for us. Strive that moral
integrity and spiritual values will mature so that, unlike other institutions in the history of this world, Hartland Institute will be stronger
each unfolding year of its existence.

3. I pray that future presidents and their administrative teams will
ever remember the holy purpose for which God has called them to
these responsibilities, that they will be men and women of prayer and
daily study of the Word, that they will seek to direct Hartland institute according to the footsteps of Jesus Christ.

4. I challenge the students to cherish the privilege Hartland provides
to be trained in a model Christian school. Each student shares with
the Constituency, the Board, the administration and the staff the
responsibility not only to maintain, but to increase the integrity of
Hartland's goals and purposes. Students honor this college only as
they selflessly follow the promptings of the Holy Spirit. Every graduate must stand ready to serve at his alma mater if ever required. I
believe that the best choices for constituency, board, administrative

and staff possibilities, will often be our faithful graduates who have a God-given responsibility to continue the upward progress of Hartland Institution, to keep it from subtle compromises, to protect against the intrusion of winds of doctrine, and to uphold the God-ordained standards that protect against worldliness and wickedness. Of course we will ever welcome dedicated and qualified constituents and board members from non-Hartland graduates, appreciative of the aims and mission of Hartland.

5.  I pray that the achievements of the past will pale into insignificance compared with the mighty works that God will in future days accomplish through Hartland, and that its staff and students will prepare their lives to be ready to receive the latter rain. We have barely touched the resources of the internet, radio, television, CDs and DVDs as great witnessing tools and we must not neglect any viable way to spread the gospel. We have worked in ninety-eight countries but these represent less than half of the nations of the world.

6.  I pray above everything else that all who have been touched by Hartland will have been led closer to Jesus through His saving grace.

7.  Finally, I pray that my prediction of twenty years ago, that if Hartland is still functioning fifty years after its establishment it will likely be in apostasy, will prove false. I pray that the Lord Jesus Christ, the Hope of our salvation, will have returned long before 2033 to claim His faithful saints; and if, because of any lack of readiness in God's saints, this has not taken place, that Hartland will have gone from strength to strength, from might to might, from holiness unto holiness as its staff and students become leading lights for the completion of the gospel commission and for the salvation of the inhabitants of this planet. This will be the certain result if all are united in truth and sanctification by grace and are empowered by the reception of the latter rain.

COLIN DAVID STANDISH
RAPIDAN, VIRGINIA
JUNE, 2003

# 28 Hartland Memories

*The system of education instituted at the beginning of the world was to be a model for man throughout all aftertime. As an illustration of its principles a model school was established in Eden, the home of our first parents. The Garden of Eden was the schoolroom, nature was the lesson book, the Creator Himself was the instructor, and the parents of the human family were the students.*
—Education, 20

*Entrance to Hartland Institute of Health & Education*

*Hartland Hall, the main College and Administrative building of Hartland Institute.*

*The primary entrance to Hartland Hall, referred to as the "Mansion."*

*Elder Colin Standish, Blue Mountain Academy seminar. 1982*

*The first Board of Health Ministries East. Front row:Hal Mayer; Glenn Hoffman (Chairman); Colin Standish. Back row: Dr. James Drexler; Lester Ortiz; Darwin Heisey; Dr. Raymond Moore. Absent: Dr. Josephine Cunnington Edwards.*

*The first staff at Hartland Institute of Health and Education. 1983*

*Log Manor, a rebuilt log cabin, has served as both staff and student housing over the years.*

*Dr. & Mrs. Carl Anderson, early volunteer staff at the college. Dr. Anderson taught early church history. 1984*

*The first Bible Conference, held in Ontario, CA. December 1983*

*Regina Young (left), here pictured with Betsy Mayer, was the first graduate of Hartland College. She was a Junior transfer.*

*Timothy Bailey (r) leads a team of fellow students in Hartland's first summer colporteur program.*

*Elder Milo Sawval, first Director of Development. 1983*

*First College Choir, under the direction of Betsy Mayer.*

*Gerald Hammon, with family, was the first cafeteria director.*

Earl & Darlis Schoonard. Earl
was the first director of plant
maintenance. 1983

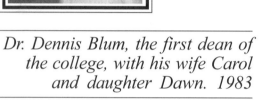

Dr. Dennis Blum, the first dean of
the college, with his wife Carol
and daughter Dawn. 1983

Elder Colin & Cheryl
Standish with son Nigel.
1983

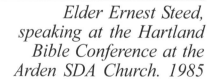

Elder Ernest Steed,
speaking at the Hartland
Bible Conference at the
Arden SDA Church. 1985

*Hal and Betsy Mayer, two of the pioneers at Hartland Institute. 1983*

*Lori Nelson (L) training health guests in healthy cooking in the early years of the Hartland Wellness Center. 1985*

*Dr. John Goley with wife Kathy and daughter Jennifer. Dr. Goley was the 1st chairman of the Hartland College Health Department.*

*The first four-year graduates. 1987*

*Groundbreaking for the Wellness Center. From L to R - Rep. Frank Slaughter, Richard Mayer (chairman of Hartland Board of Directors) Dr. Warren Peters (Director of the Health Center); Dr. Colin Standish (President of Hartland Institute); O. D. McKee (major donor); Linda Ball (head nurse, Hartland Health Center). 1986*

*The front of the Hartland Wellness Center - under construction. 1988*

*Elder Marc Coleman (Class of 1988), while a student training in block laying for the Wellness Center as his vocational training.*

*The first two Hartland medical doctors: Dr. Warren Peters (L) and Dr. Gayle Wilson.*

*Dr. Gayle Wilson praying with Edna Martin, Hartland's first convert. She was a Menonite before conversion. Unfortunately she died of advanced cancer 2 years later, 1985.*

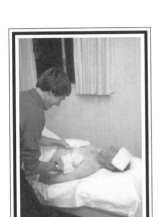

*Pastor Mike Thompson (Class of 1991) giving a hydrotherapy treatment in the late 1980s.*

*The first camp meeting, held in the front circle. Nearly 1000 attended.*

*Pastor Joe Crews baptizing a young man at Hartland's first camp meeting.*

*Dr. Ralph Larson, speaking at Hartland's annual camp meeting. 1989*

*The first issue of Last Generation magazine, published on campus by staff and students.*

*Pastoral Evangelism graduate, Raymond DeCarlo.*

*The Hartland Choir sang at the 1990 General Conference. That fall the choir became an official outreach of the college and began weekend tours.*

*Hartland Publications and Stewardship Ministries share this spacious building near the Pavilion.*

*One of the newly-constructed dormitories on the campus. This one of two serves the men.*

*The Pavilion on the campus of Hartland Institute used for camp meetings, convocations, health and education seminars, graduations, and other major events.*

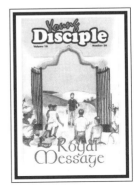

*Bros. Colin (L) and Russell Standish during a round table dialogue at a camp meeting seminar.*

*Young Disciple, then based at Hartland, publishes quarterly magazines for ages 10-15.*

*The Hartland farm not only provides a rich seasonal harvest for use on the campus, it provides a blessing for the well-rounded education of the students.*

*Hartland College Graduates of 2002.*

*Students from many nations attend Hartland to: "Go ye unto all the world . . ."*

*Hartland Students Lacey Klump and Brian Beavers, teach children in the mission fields of Thailand.*

*Joe and Elsa Willis begin Maranatha Medical Ministries in Honduras, providing internship opportunities for many students.*

*Bible teacher Peter Gregory with Hartland staff and students conducting evangelistic meetings in India.*

*Australian student Anthony Van Duyn prepares books at Hartland Publications as part of his work study.*

*Hartland College students hard at work in one of the many health-related courses.*

*Mr. Jeff Gordon, cafeteria director, preparing for the annual Thanksgiving dinner. 2001*

## About the Author

**COLIN STANDISH** was born in Newcastle, Australia, in 1933. He obtained his teaching diploma from Avondale College in 1951. He was barely 18 years of age, and was appointed to one-teacher primary (elementary) schools in rural areas of New South Wales. Colin taught for two years in Burringbar and one year at Mullumbimby, on the far north coast of New South Wales.

Upon completing three years of primary-school teaching each, he decided to become a high-school teacher. With this goal in view, he commenced studies at Sydney University, completing a major in history and undertaking an honors degree in psychology. The field of study, which required both a theoretical and an empirical thesis, was in the area of learning theory. Colin continued in this area, obtaining his Master of Arts degree with honors in 1961, and completed his Doctor of Philosophy in 1964. In 1967, he completed the Masters degree in Education. All these qualifications were completed at the University of Sydney.

In 1965, Colin was appointed Chairman of the Department of Education at Avondale College. Also he has held the post of Academic Dean at West Indies College (1970), President of West Indies College (1970—73), Chairman of the Department of Psychology, Columbia Union College (1973-74), President of Columbia Union College (1974—78), Dean of Weimar College (1978—83), and is currently President of Hartland Institute in Virginia.

When given the opportunity to establish the Christian college at Weimar Institute in 1978, Colin enthusiastically accepted the post. He had taught the principles of Christian education in each college where he served, and saw Weimar College as a challenge, where the validity of the principles of Christian education for modern times could be demonstrated. There, a program of academic excellence was combined with biblical principles of vocational training, in which students are educated in specific skills. Students are also rightly trained in outreach ministry.

In 1983 Colin was invited to become the Foundational President of Hartland Institute, the goals of which are to educate young people to offer their lives selflessly in service for God and man. The college's training is enhanced by the ministry of the wellness center, publishing house, and world mission divisions.

# Books by Colin and Russell Standish

### The Antichrist Is Here
$10.95 PB 185 pgs.
A newly updated, second edition! Colin & Russell Standish look carefully at the Scriptural identification of the Antichrist. They each have extensively researched the historical identification of past generations and are convinced the Antichrist is present on earth now. You will read undeniable evidence in support of their findings. They have taken especially those events which have transpired in the last decade & measured them in the light of Biblical prophecy. This is a "must-read" for those who are interested in Biblical prophecy and its outworking in contemporary history.

### The Big Bang Exploded
$11.95 PB 218 pgs.
The Big Bang hypothesis has held sway as the dominant explanation of the origin of the universe. It has been a remarkably enduring hypothesis, yet the determined efforts of scientists from many disciplines to provide powerful confirmation has been strikingly elusive. This challenges the Big Bang theory and Darwin's proposal of natural selection as "spent, decayed and archaic theories." This book seriously addresses some of the most startling challenges to this theory of origins. The authors boldly present evidence which they assert supports, far more closely, the fiat creation concept than the evolutionary model. This is another of the increasing challenges which evolutionary scientists must address if their credibility is not to be seriously undermined.

### Education for Excellence
$11.95 PB 176 pgs.
In the ministry of the apostle Paul, the culture, philosophy & education of paganism was confronted by the principles of God-given education. Though his world was under the political rulership of Rome, Greece still controlled the mind, therefore the educational processes. As in that day, it is necessary for us to define clearly the differences between pagan and Christian education. "For the wisdom of this world is foolishness to God. For it is written, He taketh the wise in their own craftiness." (1 Cor. 3:19) It goes directly to

the word of God for the educational principles for the sons & daughters of the King of the Universe.

## The Entertainment Syndrome
$8.95 PB 126 pgs.

Never in our history has there been such a systematic attempt to destroy the minds of a generation. Perceptive Christians recognize that entertainment is the key to the final efforts of Satan to destroy the witness of the faithful. It may be the single most dangerous element in the disruption of productive lives in modern society. There is hardly a woe in the world that cannot be directly connected to entertainment. This book explores how this large increase in entertainment impacts the physical, emotional, social, intellectual & spiritual life of the human race. In graphic detail, the authors portray what can be the outcome of even the simplest forms of what many might consider to be "innocent" entertainment.

## The Evangelical Dilemma
$10.95 PB 222 pgs.

Rarely has a book in modern times so thoroughly examined the teachings of Evangelical Protestantism as does the *Evangelical Dilemma*. Written from a supportive perspective, but with a directness that every Evangelical will recognize. Beleaguered on every side by changing world expectations, by the inroads of the Evangelical movement, by the tantalizing enigmas of the Charismatic movement and by the uncertainty of pluralism, there has never been a more urgent time for an honest review of the past, present and future of Evangelical Protestantism. The authors not only expose the dilemma of modern-day Evangelicalism, but also offer clear Biblical solutions. This is a must book for Evangelical clergy and laity.

## Georgia Sits On Grandpa's Knee (R. Standish)
$7.95 PB 86 pgs.

Pastor Russell Standish, an Australian physician who specialized in internal medicine, spent many years in Southeast Asia as a medical missionary. His work took him to many fascinating points in Asia. His family shared his experiences. He has only one grandchild, Georgia, born May 29, 1993. She lives in Michigan with her parents Timothy & Jean. During Russell's frequent visits to the U.S., his great delight is to visit his little granddaughter. She loves to sit on her grandpa's knee & hear stories of "the old times" when her daddy was a little boy in Australia, Malaysia, Thailand, England &

Singapore, and had such exciting times. Of course, it is Russell's delight to relate to Georgia these tales of a family era now past, sharing the joys of life together as a family.

## God's Solution for Depression, Guilt & Mental Illness
$12.95 PB 229 pgs.
The authors believe that true biblical principles have the most complete answer to the escalating emotional & social issues confronting society today, that true mental health is dependent upon a right relationship with God. At a time when humanistic and New Age concepts are dominating psychological theory and practice, this powerful book argues with great persuasiveness that God, the Creator of man, is interested in every aspect of His created beings. Therefore, the most perfect answers to man's physical, emotional, social, intellectual, & spiritual needs are to be found in the Word of God. You will find the insights of this book to be of inestimable value to their Christian experience.

## Grandpa, You're Back! (R. Standish)
$9.95 PB 128 pgs.
"Yes, Georgia, I am. It is so good to be once more with my dear granddaughter. You are very special to your Grandpa because you are the only child of my dear son, Timothy. "But let me take a look at you. How you have grown! Now you are 9 years old. I have lots more stories I can tell you. You can sit on Grandpa's knee like you used to do, but probably you will just want to sit and listen. "Since I last wrote you stories in Georgia Sits on Grandpa's Knee, Grandpa has been to many countries around the world telling of Jesus' love. I wonder if you have heard of all these countries. I have been here in America preaching and also to Honduras and El Salvador in Central America. Georgia, please get your atlas and I'll show you where these various countries are. I want you to know the various countries of the world for one day God may ask you to be a missionary in some interesting far-off land. I've also travelled to Dominican Republic in the Caribbean Sea and to Bolivia, Ecuador and Brazil in South America. I have preached in Kenya and Uganda in Africa, England, Macedonia, Germany, Sweden, Spain and Portugal in Europe, India, Singapore and Malaysia in Asia and New Zealand as well as Australia. "There are so many stories I could tell. I'll choose some that I think you will find very interesting. "Sit down and I'll tell you a story ..."

**Gwanpa and Nanny's Home** (R. Standish)
"I am Ella Marie Rankin. I want to tell you about Gwanpa's and Nanny's home. But I have a problem! You see, I'm only three and I haven't yet learnt to write. So my Gwanpa is writing my story for me. I can speak and tell him the things I like. One day I hope I can write my own book. Won't that be good?" So begins a book that Russell Standish wrote for his granddaughter.

**Holy Relics or Revelation**
$14.95 PB 300 pgs.
For the devout Christian, faith is in the revealed Word. When Biblical archaeology confirms the Scripture, it stirs the heart. Biblical archaeologists have gathered data with painstaking effort. Their work proves the accuracy of the Bible. Yet mostly within a single decade, Ron Wyatt had sought out & claimed the most amazing Biblical sites & relics. In this book, the Standish Brothers examine the Wyatt claims in-depth, going beyond his videotaped claims. These findings serve as a benchmark upon which Ron Wyatt's "discoveries" can be more carefully evaluated.

**Liberty in the Balance**
$12.95 PB 263 pgs.
The bloodstained pathway to religious and civil liberty faces its greatest test in 200 years. The United States "Bill of Rights" lifted the concept of liberty far beyond the realm of toleration to an inalienable right for all citizens. Yet for a century & a half, some searchers of prophetic utterances of John the Revelator have foretold a time just prior to the return of Christ when all these most cherished freedoms will be wrenched from the citizens of the United States. Further, it was understood that the U.S. would enforce its coercive edicts upon the rest of the world. This book from the Standish Brothers traces the courageous battle for freedom, a battle stained with the lives of many martyrs.

**The Lord's Day**
$15.95 PB 310 pgs.
The Lord's Day is a term used only once in Scripture. John the beloved declared, "I was in the Spirit on the Lord's day" (Revelation 1:10). In his famous encyclical *Dies Domini*, Pope John Paul II commenced with these words, "The Lord's Day–as Sunday was called from apostolic times." To many Protestants, this was an unexpected and much approved declaration from the pontiff of the

Roman Catholic Church. Protestants were not accustomed to hear such a declaration issuing forth from Roman Catholic sources, let alone from the supreme pontiff himself. The issue of the apostolic origin of Sunday worship had often been a contentious one between Roman Catholics and Protestants. The pope used words that had issued forth previously almost exclusively from Protestant sources. It was not uncommon, especially during the 19th and early 20th centuries for Roman Catholics to challenge this declaration of Protestant authors. Indeed the Roman Catholic Church routinely denied any apostolic link to Sunday observance as the special day of Christian worship. Roman Catholic apologists declared that there was no Biblical nor apostolic link between Sunday observance and the early Christian Church. Boldly, Roman Catholic theologians had claimed that the origin of the 1st day as the Christians' Lord's Day had its source in a decision voted by the Council of Laodicea held in the 4th century.

### Modern Bible Translations Unmasked
$10.95 PB 228 pgs.
This is a fascinating book that will challenge the reader to consider two very serious problems with modern Bible translations: first, the use of corrupted Greek manuscripts; and second, translational bias. Are modern translations designed to reinforce false teachings and erroneous gospel presentations. Does this lead to dangers for the soul salvation. Is any translation as acceptable as another. This is a must read for anyone interested the veracity and accuracy of the Word of God.

### The Mystery of Death
$10.95 PB 128 pgs.
Most people hold life precious, yet all know that death is inevitable. But what then? Some feel that it is merely a transition to a wonderfully enlightened paradise, reincarnating into another form of life or another person. Some see death as a state of unconsciousness, awaiting resurrection, or that death is eternal oblivion. Like the ancient Greeks, there are those who believe that the soul is immortal and externally preexisted the body. Pagan or Christian, the opinions vary widely. In this book, the history of these various concepts is reviewed and the words of Scripture are investigated for a definitive and unchallengeable answer.

**Perils of Ecumenism**
$15.95 PB 416 pgs.
The march of ecumenism seems unstoppable. From its humble roots after the first World War, with the formation of the Faith and Order Council at Edinburgh University, Scotland, and the Works and Labor Council at Oxford University, England, to the formation of the World Council of Churches in 1948 in Amsterdam, the Ecumenical Movement has gained breathtaking momentum. Further impetus to the movement was provided by the Second Vatican Council 1962-64. It would seem that only a handful of small church groups has continued to resist the power of this movement. The goals of the ecumenical movement are noble: the uniting together of the people of the world to bring peace, harmony and unity to a world that for millennia has been fragmented. The authors see the ecumenical movement as very clearly identified in Holy Scriptures as the movement devised by the arch-deceiver to beguile the inhabitants of the world.

**The Pope's Letter and Sunday Law**
$7.95 PB 116 pgs.
Unquestionably the most poignant, critical evaluation of the recent papal Apostolic Letter. Examines the Biblical foundations upon which the pope seeks to buttress his cleverly crafted letter. But even the undoubted skill of the pope & his scholarly advisors cannot mask the fallacies. The pope's assertions are in deep contradiction to the Holy Bible & the record of history. Accepting the pope's conclusions leads one into the trap of deadly error & away from the truths of Christ. John's illumination of end-times in Rev. Chapter 13 reveals a unity of two superpowers which will unite together to fearfully persecute those who will yield their will only to Christ & His truth.

**The Rapture and the Antichrist**
This book sets forth the plainest truths of Scripture directing Protestantism back to its biblical roots. It will challenge the thinking of all Christians, erase the fictions of the *Left Behind* Series, and plant the readers' spiritual feet firmly on the platform of Scripture.

**The Rapture, the End Times and the Millennium**
This book will open the minds of the readers to a clear understanding of areas of the end-time which have led to much perplexity among lay-people and theologians alike. It is also guaranteed to open to the reader biblical issues-often overlooked-which, when

understood in the light of Scripture, dispel many of the perplexities presently confronting those who are searching for a clear biblical exposition of the last cataclysmic days in which we now live.

### The Sacrificial Priest
$15.95 PB 272 pgs.

Moses, Paul and John all witnessed the splendor and majesty of the heavenly sanctuary. But beyond the sanctuary itself, Paul and John testified to the two thousand year ministry of the risen Saviour in this sanctuary. To all Christians the centrality of the sacrifice of Christ on Calvary has been the focus of their salvation hopes. But relatively few Christians have understood the equally important ministry of Christ in the heavenly sanctuary. Just as the salvation of man could not be purchased without the substitutionary sacrifice of Jesus, neither could that salvation be completed without Christ's high priestly ministry in the heavenly sanctuary. The authors provide a fascinating Biblical explanation of this little-studied ministry of Christ. They offer irrefutable evidence of the first and second apartment ministry of Jesus. As the sun sets on this world's history, they present an impelling reason for the study of this fascinating theme.

### The Second Coming
$7.95 PB 80 pgs.

The Apostle Paul refers to the second coming of Jesus as the blessed hope (Titus 2:12). As you study the New Testament you will find a central theme of hope in the return of Jesus Christ. New Testament writers presented this as the critical focus, yet soon after the death of all apostles, doubts & debates robbed the people of this assurance and brought in the pagan notion of immediate life after death. In this new updated work, Colin & Russell Standish present a "wake-up call" for every complacent Christian, despite what their belief is concerning man's state-in-death.

### Two Beasts, Three Deadly Wounds & Fourteen Popes
$16.95 PB 234 pgs.

The Book of Revelation has been characterized as a mystery. Yet the book describes itself as the "Revelation of Jesus Christ" (Rev. 1:1). A revelation is the opposite of a mystery. In this book, Russell & Colin Standish, using Scripture as its own interpreter, unravel aspects of the "mystery" and unveil a portion of the revelation. Revelation Chapter 13 presents two of the most curious beasts imaginable. The spotlight of this book is on these two apparently incomprehensible beasts–one of which receives a deadly wound in one of its heads. Prophecy stated that this mortal injury would be healed, and that the power represented by the beast would be admired worldwide.

**The Vision and God's Providence** (C. Standish)
$12.95 PB  176 pgs.
The story of Hartland Institute is the story of the struggles and triumphs, the fear and faith, the failures and successes, the timidity and courage, and the hesitations and visions of fallible men and women. In spite of human limitations, the glorious power of the Almighty God has been revealed. Not simply the achievements or accomplishments of men or women can tell the story of the initial or subsequent development of Hartland Institute, for its foundation must be attributed to God alone. Yet many men and women have had the privilege of being His humble instruments to contribute to Hartland's establishment. Some worked as the pioneer Hartland team. Others have come to continue the Institute's development, while yet others have supported Hartland's vision with prayers, encouraging words, or have given direction as constituents and Board members and by serving on Advisory Committees. Still others have contributed funds, equipment and labor. All who have assisted over the years have been crucial for the construction of a mosaic which represents an example of God's artwork. Some have passed to their rest. We honor their memory. As this book recalls divine leadings, it may at times appear as if the development had been largely free from struggle, human weakness, misunderstandings, and strong differences of opinion. All these human frailties occurred, and we cannot but wonder what God might have accomplished, had we listened perfectly to His voice. Yet despite human weakness, there has been much faith, prayer and soul searching which God has honored.

**Youth Do You Dare!** (C. Standish)
$6.95 PB 74 pgs.
If you are a young person looking for workable answers to the many issues that confront you today, this book is for you. Set in short, relevant chapters, this book addresses questions concerning the meaning of life, and how to handle the myriads of temptations that Satan places before young people today. It addresses the issue of moral purity, why it is so important, and how it can be main-

tained. We believe that you will find this a very relevant and helpful book. Our prayer is that as you read you will be challenged, and strengthened, and appreciative of the wise counsel that God has for young people.

# Other Books from Hartland Publications

**Behold the Lamb** - David Kang
$8.95 PB 107 pgs.
God's plan of redemption for this world & the preservation of the universe is revealed in the sanctuary which God constructed through Moses. Through the sanctuary & it's services, God reveals to us how He deals with & resolves the sin problem. This book explains the sanctuary service in the light of the Christian's personal experience. Why this book? Because Jesus is coming soon!

**Christ and Antichrist** - Samuel J. Cassels
$24.95 HB 348 pgs.
First published in 1846 by a well-known Presbyterian minister, who calls this book "not sectarian, but a Christian and Protestant work." He hoped that the removal of obstacles might result in a more rapid spread of the Gospel. He saw one of these obstacles as Antichristianity," by which term he described the Papal system.

**Distinctive Vegetarian Cuisine** - Sue M. Weir
$14.95 PB 329 pgs.
100% vegan cooking, with no animal products—no meat, milk, eggs, cheese, or even honey. Even more healthful ... no irritating spices or condiments are used. Most of the ingredients can be found at your local market. Additional nutritional information and helpful hints. Make your dinner table appealing to the appetite!

**Food for Thought** - Susan Jen
$10.95 PB 160 pgs.
Where does the energy which food creates come from? What kinds of foods are the most conductive to robust health and well being in all dimensions of our life? What is a balanced diet? Written by a healthcare professional, this book examines the food we prepare for our table.

**Group Think** - Horace E. Walsh
$5.95 PB 96 pgs.
Find out how a state of groupthink (or group dynamics) has often contributed to disaster in secular & spiritual matters, like the role of

Hebrew groupthink in the rejection & ultimate crucifixion of the Son of God. Or the Ecumenical Movement that seeks to unite the minds of dedicated men so much that their passion is to build one great super church following Rome.

### Heroes of the Reformation - Hagstotz & Hagstotz
$14.95 PB 320 pgs.
This volume brings together a comprehensive picture of the leaders of the Reformation who arose all over Europe. The authors of this volume have made a sincere endeavor to bring the men of Protestantism alive in the hearts of this generation.

### His Mighty Love - Ralph Larson
$9.95 PB 159 pgs.
21 evangelistic sermons! Every doctrine of the Bible is simply an answer to the question, "How does the love of God relate to this particular question or problem?" Every doctrine is further evidence that God is love! Divided into three sections with seven individual sermons each. Subjects range from "If God Is Almighty, Why Does He Permit Sin?" to "The Unpardonable Sin."

### History of the Gunpowder Plot - Philip Sidney
$13.95 PB 303 pgs.
Originally published on the 300th anniversary of the November 5th, 1605, plot aimed at the destruction of the English Realm, Philip Sydney's account of one of the most audacious conspiracies ever known to the ancient or modern world is filled with royal intrigue of the court of James the First, Rome-backed Jesuit infiltrators and an aristocratic little band of traitors. The failed plot became part of English popular culture.

### The History of Protestantism - J. A. Wylie
$99.95 PB 4 Volumes
*The History of Protestantism* by J. A. Wylie is an incredibly inspiring work. It pulls back the divine curtain and reveals God's hand in the affairs of His church during the Protestant Reformation. Through the centuries, the sacrifices and victories of God's faithful people have often been obscured and forgotten. Now once again, you can read the fascinating story of how truth triumphed over error, principle over falsehood, and light over darkness. Your heart will be stirred by the lives of Protestant heroes, and your mind captivated

by God's simple means to counteract the intrigues of its enemies in both church and state. Though this book reads like you are right there, it often lets you watch from heaven's perspective, and opens to your mind to the highest thoughts and feelings. You will sense the unfolding drama as told in the lives and work of God fearing and courageous men and women. As God's church faces the last days, this compelling book has unique appeal and relevance to all who love the truth. This book will be a blessing to adults as well as children who enjoy reading great themes. Now that Wylie's The History of Protestantism is back in print again, the rich treat between the covers of this book awaits your eyes and mind, to bring you many hours of great history, fascinating people, and thoughtful reflection as you relive the scenes of this most eventful era.

**History of the Reformation of the 16th Century** - J. d'Aubigne'
$19.95 PB 876 pgs.
In history and in prophecy, the Word of God portrays the long continued conflict between truth and error. Today we see an alarming lack of understanding in the Protestant Church concerning the cause and effect of the Reformation. This reprinted masterpiece pulls back the curtain of history and divine providence to reveal the true catalyst for the Reformation—God's Word and His Holy Spirit.

**History of the Reformation in the Time of Calvin** - d'Aubigne'
$129.95 4 Vol.
The renovation of the individual, of the Church, and of the human race, is the theme. If the Holy Ghost kindles the lamp of truth in man, it is (according to Calvin) to the end that the entire man should be transformed. In the Kingdom of Christ, he says, it is only the new man that flourishes and has any vigor, and whom we ought to take into account. This renovation is, at the same time, an enfranchisement; and we might assign, as a motto to the Reformation accomplished by Calvin, as well as to apostolical Christianity itself, these words of Jesus Christ: The truth shall make you free (John 8:32).

**History of the Waldenses** - J. A. Wylie
$12.95 PB 191 pgs.
During the long centuries of papal supremacy, the Waldenses defied the crushing power of Rome and rejected its false doctrines and human traditions. This stalwart people cherished and preserved the pure Word of God. It is fitting that this edition of their history should

be reprinted to keep alive the spirit and knowledge of this ancient people. May it rekindle in the heart of all God's people the love of the truth and an unflinching courage to stand, whatever the cost.

**Hus the Heretic** - Poggius the Papist
$9.95 PB 78 pgs.
One of the greatest of Reformers in history was John Hus. His pious life & witness during his trial & martyrdom convinced many of the priests & church leaders of his innocence & the justice of his cause. Poggius was the papal legate who delivered the summons to Hus to appear at the council of Constance, then participated member. Hus was given a safe conduct by the emperor Sigismund which he cowardly broke in deference to pressure from Hus' enemies. This book consists of letters from Poggius to his friend Nikolai, and describes in living detail the trial & burning of Hus. So potent was John Hus' humble testimony contrasted with the amazing rudeness & injustice of the priests & cardinals, that even some of his ardent foes became his defenders.

**The Law and the Sabbath** - Allen Walker
$9.95 PB 149 pgs.
If Christians are under grace and not the law, how can the Sabbath be relevant today? A fierce controversy is swirling around the role the Ten Commandments should play in the church of the 21st Century. With a foreword by the late Elder Joe Crews, here is a book that dares to examine the Bible's own answers—with unfailing scriptural logic and a profound appreciation for the doctrine of righteousness by faith.

**The Method of Grace** - John Flavel
$14.95 PB 458 pgs.
In this faithful reprint, John Flavel thoroughly outlines the work of God's Spirit in applying the redemptive work of Christ to the believer. Readers will search their hearts and find their faith challenged and enriched. In the true Puritan tradition, a clearly defined theology is delivered with evangelistic fervor, by an author urgently concerned about the eternal destiny of the human soul.

**My Escape from the Auto de Fe** - Don Fernando de la Mina
$9.95 PB 112 pgs.
In the difficult days of the Reformation in Spain, Nobleman Don Fernando de la Mina was arrested by the Inquisitors and sentenced

to death for "heresy." Because of his reformed beliefs, he was about to be burned at the stake at the Auto de Fe´ (act of faith), when, through several incredible miracles of Providence, he made his escape. Disguised and unrecognized, even by his fiance´ who was also suspected of reform ideas, Don Fernando attempted to rescue his beloved and flee with her to France. This captivating story is full of intrigue, suspense, humor and hope. With every step there is new danger. It will thrill and amaze you, and strengthen your faith in the protecting hand over God's faithful believers.

**The Reformation in Spain** - Thomas M'Crie
$13.95 PB 272 pgs.
The boldness with which Luther attacked the abuses and the authority of the Church in Rome in the 16th Century attracted attention throughout Christendom. Luther's writings, along with the earlier ones of Erasmus, gained a foothold with a Spanish people hungry for the truth. Thomas M'Crie makes a case for a Spain free of the religious errors and corruptions that ultimately dried up the resources and poisoned the fountains of a great empire.

**Romanism and the Reformation** - H. Grattan Guinness
$12.95 PB 217 pgs.
The Reformation of the 16th Century, which gave birth to Protestantism, was based on Scripture. It gave back to the world the Bible. Such Reformation work needs to be done again. The duty of diffusing information on the true character and history of "Romanism and the Reformation" is one which presses on God's faithful people in these days.

**Strange Fire** - Barry Harker
$11.95 PB 206 pgs.
The Olympic games are almost universally accepted as a great international festival of peace, sportsmanship, and friendly competition. Yet the games are riddled with conflict, cheating, and objectionable competitiveness. Discover the disturbing truth about the modern Olympics and the role of Christianity in the rise of this neo-pagan religion.

**Truth Triumphant** - Benjamin George Wilkinson
$14.95 PB 419 pgs.
The prominence given to the "Church in the Wilderness" in the Scriptures establishes without argument its existence and empha-

sizes its importance. The doctrines of the primitive Christian church spread to Ireland, Scotland and Wales. The same challenges exist today with the Remnant Church in its final controversy against the powers of evil to show the holy, unchanging message of the Bible.

**Who Are These Three Angels?** - Jeff Wehr
$6.95 PB 126 pgs.
Millions believe angels exist. Many have encountered them in the last few years, but few truly understand the nature and purpose of these heavenly beings. The messages of three holy angels unfold for us events that are soon to take place. Their warning is not to be taken lightly. They tell of political and religious movements that signal the soon return of Jesus.

# True Education History Series
# from Hartland Publications

**The Waldenses - The Church in the Wilderness**
$7.95 PB 72 pgs.
The faithful Waldenses in their mountain retreats were married in a spiritual sense to God who promised, "I will betroth thee unto me in faithfulness and thou shalt know the Lord" (Hosea 2:20). No invention of Satan could destroy their union with God. "Who shall separate us from the love of Christ? shall tribulation, or distress, or persecution, or famine, or nakedness, or peril, or sword?" (Romans 8:35). The world would see that even death could not separate the Waldenses from their God. Follow the history of these people as they are compared to the dedicated eagle parents.

**David Livingstone - The Pathfinder** - Basil Matthews
$8.95 PB 112 pgs.
Like most boys and girls, David Livingstone wondered what he would become when he grew up. He had heard of a brave man who was a missionary doctor in China. He also learned that this Dr. Gulztoff had a Hero, Jesus, who had come to people as a healer and missionary. David learned all about this great Physician. Now that he was soon to be a young man, David felt that the finest thing in the whole world for him was to follow in the same way and be a medical missionary. David would say to himself, "The great God had an only Son, and He was sent to earth as a missionary. It is something to be a follower in the wake of the only Model Missionary that ever appeared among men." That was David's quest, that was his plan. Between these pages you shall see how he made his good wish come true.

**Missionary Annuls - Memoir of Robert Moffat** - M. L. Wilder
$7.95 PB 64 pgs.
Robert Moffat first heard from his wise and pious mother's lips that there were heathen in the world and of the efforts of Christians sharing the knowledge of a Savior who could raise them out of their base degradation. An intense desire took possession of him to

serve God in some marked manner but how that would be, he did not know. Through a series of providential circumstances and in God good time, the London Society accepted Robert Moffat as one of their missionaries. In 1816, he embarked on his first trip and also got his first glimpse of heathen Africa. This book will inspire the young and old as you read the many trials, disappointments, as well as the triumphs, and the wondrous miracles that God can accomplish when one is fully surrendered to the Lord.

**HARTLAND PUBLICATIONS** was established in 1984 as a conservative, self supporting Protestant publishing house. We publish Bible-based books and produce media for Christians of all ages, to help them in the development of their personal characters, always giving glory to God in preparation for the soon return of our Lord and Savior, Christ Jesus. We are especially dedicated to the reprinting of significant books on Protestant history that might otherwise go out of circulation. Hartland Publications supports and promotes other Christian publishers and media producers who are consistent with biblical principles of truth and righteousness. We are seeking to arouse the spirit of true Protestantism, one that is based on the Bible and the Bible only, thus awakening the world to a sense of the value and privilege of the religious liberty that we currently enjoy.

Office hours: 9:00 am, to 5:00 p.m. Mon.— Thurs.,
9:00 a.m. to 12:00 noon Fri. (Eastern time)

You may order by telephone, fax, mail, email or on the website.

Payments in $US
by check, money order, most credit cards.

Order line: 1-800-774-3566
FAX 1-540-672-3568

Website: www.hartlandpublications.com
Email:sales@hartlandpublications.org